Purse c

GU00949897

Purse or Wallet?

Gender inequalities and income distribution within families on benefits

JACKIE GOODE
CLAIRE CALLENDER
RUTH LISTER

POLICY STUDIES INSTITUTE

UNIVERSITY OF WESTMINSTER

PSI is a wholly owned subsidiary of the University of Westminster

© **Policy Studies Institute 1998**

A CIP catalogue record of this book is available from the British Library.

ISBN 0 85374 749 0
PSI Report No. 853

Typeset by Policy Studies Institute
Printed by Athenæum Press Ltd, Gateshead, Tyne & Wear

Policy Studies Institute is one of Europe's leading research organiations undertaking studies of economic, industrial and social policy and the workings of political institutions. The Institute is a registered charity and is not associated with any political party, pressure group or commercial interest.

For further information contact
Policy Studies Institute, 100 Park Village East, London NW1 3SR
Tel: 0171 468 0468   Fax: 0171 388 0914 Email: pubs@psi.org. uk

Contents

Tables

Acknowledgements

We would like to express our appreciation of the excellent support provided by Barbara Ballard, Principal Research Manager at the Joseph Rowntree Foundation. Our gratitude goes to her, to the members of the Advisory Group who gave so generously of their time and expertise, and to the women and men who were interviewed, whose generosity and forbearance in discussing intimate and often painful areas of their lives elicited our admiration and thanks.

Jackie Goode
Researcher, Social Sciences Department,
Loughborough University

Claire Callender
Senior Research Fellow
Policy Studies Institute

Ruth Lister
Professor of Social Policy
Loughborough University

Executive summary

AIMS

This study, funded by the Joseph Rowntree Foundation, of the distribution of income within low income families, was based on separate in-depth interviews with partners in 31 couples. It examined the impact on distribution patterns of the payment of in-work and out-of-work means-tested benefits to fathers and mothers. The study's aims were to investigate:

- men's and women's perceptions of their incomes from different sources;
- the factors affecting the allocation of household income;
- the meanings individuals attributed to distribution patterns; and
- gender differences in the impact of these patterns on the material and psychological well-being of individuals.

The feasibility of different ways of splitting means-tested benefits between partners, including the retention of joint assessment but splitting payment between partners, has been floated in the past as potentially beneficial. There have also been suggestions to pay in-work benefit through the pay packet. The study explored attitudes towards these options, and examined their implications for the distribution of income within families.

Perceptions and uses of income by source

Child Benefit was positively valued by men and women, and was allocated to children either directly or via household expenditure.

Earning conferred entitlement to individual spending, although this entitlement was enacted differently by men and women.

Family Credit (FC) was positively valued by men and women, despite a perception that it enabled employers to pay inadequate wages. Mistrust of employers was translated into spontaneous support for the idea of a minimum wage. Women controlled FC, which they allocated to the family. They valued FC highly as a weekly budgeting tool. There was little evidence of a sense of stigma for men or women from claiming this benefit in contrast to the degree of stigma experienced by Income Support (IS)/income-related Jobseeker's Allowance (JSA) recipients.

Family income derived wholly from benefit was subject to multiple definitions of 'ownership'. It was seen as conferring on the man an entitlement to spend by virtue of being the recipient; as owned by the family with no individual components; and as not conferring 'entitlement' at all, because it was perceived as rightfully belonging to tax-paying wage-earners rather than to the couples who received it.

The change of title of Income Support to Jobseeker's Allowance appeared to reinforce the practice of men claiming. Couples trying to create a manageable shared pattern of combining caring for their family with paid employment were to some extent being inhibited from doing so because of a perceived requirement conclusively to nominate separate responsibilities.

Individual and collective expenditure

The study distinguished between individual and collective expenditure and consumption. Individuals' 'personal spending' and 'going without' were examined.

Men prioritised personal spending money more highly than did women, and were less able than women to give specific examples of 'going without'. Both men and women saw responsibility for ensuring that children's material needs were met as the women's domain. Women typically took responsibility for vigilant restraint over both their own and their partners' spending, going without clothing, food and toiletries in order to prioritise children's needs.

Spending, both directly and on credit, was found to be 'gendered' not only in terms of the particular items of expenditure but also in the way in which the categories of individual and collective expenditure were perceived and enacted by those engaged in the spending. Couples' own perceptions legitimated men's personal spending and defined women's collective expenditure, for example on children, as personal. In practice, therefore, the distinction between individual and collective expenditure was not as clear-cut as delineated in previous research.

DISTRIBUTION PATTERNS

The distinction between individual and collective expenditure was nevertheless one which enabled an assessment to be made of relative benefit. Couples divided into three distinct groups according to the balance of material benefit and disadvantage between the partners:

- an egalitarian group of 12 couples, in which women were responsible for financial management but couples shared financial control. Material benefits and disadvantages were evenly balanced, and expenditure by credit was jointly executed and for collective advantage.
- a traditional group of 14 couples, in which women managed the finances, but regular 'earmarked' personal spending money for men meant that they were privileged in relatively modest but real ways. Credit use was confined to the social fund and 'loan sharks' but was primarily used for spending on children and the household.

- a male-dominated group of five couples, in which men were individual beneficiaries to a significantly greater degree than women, and were aided in this by using commercial credit and other 'new forms of money'.

Overall, women had the main responsibility for managing the family's income, but men more frequently determined how it was allocated. Male control was a crucial feature of the most inegalitarian distribution patterns. A contributory factor was men's use of credit and other 'new forms of money', which effectively subverted women's financial management.

Women reported far higher levels of stress and worry in relation to family finances than men. Men acknowledged that their wives' responsibility for financial management relieved them of worry. Some women, whilst finding management responsibility burdensome, also derived peace of mind and a sense of pride from their skills as managers of a low income.

Male financial control, associated with greater female disadvantage, derived from their identity as sole breadwinner. A number of factors acted either to preserve or modify this:

- Payment of Income Support/Jobseeker's Allowance to men reinforced some couples' agreed commitment to, and joint reconstruction of, male breadwinner identity, through which men were privileged with personal spending money.
- Some men were ambivalent about the breadwinner identity ascribed to them but nevertheless exercised the entitlement to personal spending which it conferred. They were aided in this by: the deference paid to them by wives considerably younger than themselves; keeping their informal earnings; and accessing commercial forms of credit.
- Other men who ideally wanted to be sole breadwinners in fact perceived breadwinning as a joint activity because of the kind of labour market opportunities available to them and to their partners.
- Some women derived financial control from having benefit income paid directly to them, either formerly as a lone parent, or from current experience of being the recipient

of Family Credit. This degree of female financial control meant in some cases that women effectively vetoed male spending on credit as a condition of their partnership.

Important findings were the impact of life-cycle factors and the greater salience in some instances of women's attitudes in determining distribution patterns.

METHODS OF PAYING SOCIAL SECURITY BENEFITS

Men and women spontaneously identified a need, in relation to some families reliant on benefit, to protect the interests of children against men's personal spending, and saw payment of benefit to women as serving this end. The minimal support from women for Income Support/Jobseeker's Allowance to be paid wholly to them came from those who had experienced independent benefit income, and those in the least egalitarian households. Couples also opposed the idea of IS/JSA being split between partners, although they recognised it might in some cases protect women and children. Most expressed a desire to preserve the identity of benefit income as money for the family. Men and women feared that if this were replaced with a principle of individual ownership, men might exercise this entitlement to the detriment of the family as a whole.

There was considerable opposition to the idea of paying Family Credit through the pay packet. Men cited: mistrust of employers; the positive aspects of women's receipt of family credit within their current patterns of financial management; and the risk of Family Credit being swallowed up by male-incurred debt. Women cited the advantages of current methods of payment, which gave them a guaranteed weekly income, paid directly to them, available in cash at the local Post Office, and separate from their partner's wages. Women in inegalitarian households for whom Family Credit was the only income they had access to, were particularly opposed.

POLICY IMPLICATIONS

- Although the study does not reveal strong support for the individual payment of Income Support/income-related Jobseeker's Allowance, it suggests that it could be important for a minority of women.
- A more flexible benefits system which would facilitate a dual earner model, and make it easier to take part-time work, might better suit some couples on benefit and make it more likely that they would be able to get off benefit.
- Men's and women's attitudes towards Family Credit not only cast serious doubt on any proposal to replace the benefit with some form of tax credit, but also confirmed the importance of a minimum wage.
- The study underlined the importance of Child Benefit and of money for children being paid direct to the caring parent. This suggests that proposals for both a minimum wage and for an earned income tax credit should incorporate a significant increase in Child Benefit to avoid any unfortunate gendered side-effects of such policies: in the former case, where the family's main income in one-earner couples comes from the man's wages, a pay rise could lead to a cut in his partner's Family Credit, and in the latter, to protect some of the money currently paid directly to mothers to meet family needs.

Chapter 1

Introduction

This report is about the distribution of income within low income families. It is based on a study, funded by the Joseph Rowntree Foundation, which consisted of in-depth interviews with 31 couples receiving in-work or out-of-work social security benefits. It examines the patterns of money management, control, and allocation within these families and how they can lead to gendered inequalities.

BACKGROUND TO THE STUDY

Research undertaken to date has thrown some light on the gendered patterns of management, control and allocation of social security income. It has not, however, had this as its explicit focus. It has either concentrated on gendered patterns of money management across households of differing income levels, or has focused on low income families but not explored in depth the gendered nature of the distribution of income within these families. The intention of the current study, therefore, was to build on past research in order to apply a systematic gendered analysis to the study of the distribution of income specifically in families in receipt of certain means-tested social security benefits, at a time when a growing proportion of the population has become reliant on such benefits.

Pahl's (1980, 1989) work has been particularly influential in developing our understanding of intra-family income distribution and in revealing the hidden and unequal burden of poverty which can result from the uneven distribution of income within the family. In *Money and Marriage* (1989), Pahl's study of 102 couples, she identified four patterns of money management together with four main patterns of control. These, she found, were linked with the allocation of resources and with power in decision-making. The main money allocative systems she identified were:

- *wife management or whole wage,* where one partner, usually the wife, takes full responsibility for managing all the household finances except for the personal spending money of the other partner. This system was commonly found among low income families.
- *an allowance system,* characterised by separate spheres of responsibility. The husband gives his wife a fixed amount of money or housekeeping allowance every week or month. The husband has access to the main source of income while the wife has access to only the part which he chooses to give her.
- *shared management or pooling,* where income is paid into and drawn out of a joint account or common kitty and both partners have access to the money. The system is based on a partnership view of marriage, although one partner is usually dependent to some extent on the other.
- *independent management,* where each partner has an income and neither has access to each other's income. Each partner has separate responsibilities for specific items of expenditure. This can resemble an allowance system except that the husband has no access to his wife's income.

Vogler (1994) developed Pahl's work, using a quantitative approach and a significantly larger sample. She demonstrated the extent of intra-household inequalities and consequent hidden deprivation. She observed that:

> *The orthodox model of households as egalitarian decision-making units, within which resources are shared equally, applies to only a fifth (20 per cent) of the households in our sample. (p241)*

She highlighted two aspects to these inequalities where women were particularly at a disadvantage: different levels of general financial deprivation (even with respect to some items of 'collective' expenditure); and unequal access to personal spending money. She found that on both counts the inequalities were greatest under female-managed and housekeeping allowance systems. She importantly showed that inequalities were inversely linked to income levels.

Vogler (1994) also explored the relationship between strategic control and differential access to money. In low income families, even where women controlled finances, they did not gain greater access to resources, unlike in higher income families where resources were under male control:

> *female-managed systems were characterised by a disjunction between strategic control over finances and access to money. Despite egalitarian or even female strategic control over finances, wives in these households experienced significantly higher levels of financial deprivation than husbands, while husbands had greater access than wives to personal spending money.* (p241)

Her findings also confirmed that

> *women are most likely to manage finances single-handedly in low-income households where financial management is likely to be a burden rather than a source of power.* (p243)

Vogler's large-scale study was important in confirming the findings of earlier, smaller scale studies (Vogler and Pahl, 1993, 1994). It also threw more light on the ways in which low income households' patterns of money management and control differed from those in other households.

RESEARCH AIMS AND OBJECTIVES

The main aim of the study was to examine the impact of the payment of social security benefits to fathers and mothers on patterns of money management and control and on individual well-being in couples with young children.

To achieve this aim, there were the following objectives:

- to explore the gendered patterns of income control, management, and allocation within families receiving social security benefits and the factors affecting these;
- to examine gender differences in the impact of these patterns on the material and psychological well-being of different family members;
- to examine the meaning and perceptions individuals attribute to such patterns;
- to investigate the utility of the management/control and collective/individual expenditure paradigms in capturing these patterns; and
- to explore how existing social security policies help to shape these patterns, the potential impact of alternative policies, and individuals' perceptions of these alternatives.

RESEARCH METHODS

The study consisted primarily of in-depth interviews with couples receiving either Jobseeker's Allowance/Income Support or Family Credit. In-depth interviews were conducted face to face with 31 couples between March and May 1997. Each partner was interviewed separately, at home, using a semi-structured interview schedule. A total of 60 individuals were interviewed because in two cases the man was unavailable. All the interviews were tape recorded, transcribed, and analysed 'manually' and using the Nud*ist computer package. The report contains extensive quotations from the interviews. To preserve confidentiality, the women, men and children have been given pseudonyms.

The purposive sample of couples was drawn from a Policy Studies Institute database of a nationally representative sample of women in Britain who had given birth in May 1995. Thus all the couples interviewed had a young child aged just under two years old. Half of the sample were receiving Family Credit and half Jobseeker's Allowance/Income Support. They were selected because 'typically' these social security benefits are paid to different household members – Family Credit to the woman, Income Support to the man.

The key characteristics of the sample are outlined in Tables 1.1 and 1.2.

Table 1.1   Key demographic characteristics of the sample

Characteristic	Number
Age	
Women	
>20	2
21–29	13
30–39	14
40–49	2
50+	0
Men	
>20	0
21–29	11
30–39	18
40–49	1
50+	1
Number of couples with	
1 child	11
2 children	12
3 children	5
4+ children	3
Duration of couples' current partnership (years)	
>2	1
2–5	18
6–10	8
11+	4
Couples' previous experience of marriage or cohabitation	
Woman had had previous partnership, man had not	6
Man had had previous partnership, woman had not	3
Both had had a previous partnership	5
Neither had had a previous partnership	17

Table 1.2   Key socio-economic characteristics of the sample

Characteristic	Number
Couples receiving social security benefit	
Income Support/Income-related Jobseeker's Allowance	15
Family Credit	16
Current employment status of partners	
Man employed, woman not employed	12
Woman employed, man not employed	4
Man and woman both employed	2
Man and woman both not employed	13
Duration of current employment (months)	
Men	
>6	1
6–12	4
13–18	3
19–24	1
25+	7
Women	
>6	1
6–12	2
13–18	1
19–24	1
25+	1
Duration of receipt of Family Credit (months)	
>6	1
6–12	5
13–18	5
24	5
Duration of current period of unemployment (months)	
Men	
>6	2
6–12	3
13–18	1
19–24	3
25+	4
Not known	2

continued

Table 1.2 continued

Characteristic	Number
Duration of current period of unemployment (months)	
Women	
>6	0
6–12	0
13–18	1
19–24	1
25+	23

OUTLINE OF THE REPORT

The next chapter examines the money coming into the households and the couples' perceptions and use of different sources of income. Chapter 3 explores the patterns of financial management and discusses the allocation systems used in the households and how these were identified and classified. Chapter 4 looks at the outcomes of these allocation systems with regards to individual and collective expenditure. Chapter 5 introduces a typology of households which is related to constructions of the 'breadwinner' ideology, while Chapter 6 develops this typology further in explaining the patterns of income distribution. Chapter 7 focuses on alternative models of social security payments and the couples' views on them, and draws on these and other findings to explore the social policy implications. Finally, Chapter 8 brings together key findings in relation to the overall aims and objectives of the study.

Chapter 2

Money entering the household

This chapter looks at the different sources of money entering the household. It examines who earns wages and who makes the benefit claim, who has access to income, and how different sources of household income are perceived and used. Gender differences are highlighted in the ways in which these sources of income are viewed and used for either individual or collective purposes, a distinction which is explored in greater depth in Chapter 4.

CHILD BENEFIT

Child Benefit is a non-means tested benefit paid to all mothers in respect of all dependent children up to the time they leave tertiary education. The rates for couples at the time of the interviews were £11.05 per week for the eldest child, and £9.00 per week for younger children. Child Benefit can be cashed or paid directly into a bank or building society account.

How Child Benefit was paid

- In 22 of the 31 couples, the woman cashed the Child Benefit by 'book' at the Post Office, usually on a weekly basis, but in two cases monthly. (This means that two-thirds of couples received Child Benefit weekly, compared to just over half of couples nationally. *1995/96 Family Resources Survey.)*

- In three couples, the man sometimes or usually cashed the book. Where the couple had done a 'role swap' and the husband used the Family Credit and the Child Benefit as housekeeping money, he would sometimes cash these benefits himself. In the other two cases, both partners said that the woman preferred the man to manage the money. The man therefore cashed the Child Benefit in addition to the Jobseeker's Allowance, and this formed part of a broader picture of male control within these households.
- In four cases, the Child Benefit was paid directly into a joint account from which the woman managed the household finances, and one woman had the Child Benefit and the Family Credit paid directly into her personal account. In one instance, the Child Benefit together with the Family Credit and the man's wages were paid directly into his account.

There was no evidence to suggest that having the Child Benefit paid directly into a bank account resulted in diminished female access to it. In one of the six cases, it was paid into the woman's own account, and in three others the joint account was only drawn upon in practice by the woman.[1] In only one case, therefore, was the Child Benefit paid into an account to which only the man had access, and this was where the woman preferred her husband to manage all the household finances.

How Child Benefit was perceived and used

Child Benefit was seen as earmarked for children. Personal spending particularly was seen as prohibited from this source, constituting what one man described as 'robbing the bairns'.

Some couples referred to better-off extended family members putting the Child Benefit into a savings account for the child, or giving it to the child as pocket money, a practice that these couples could not emulate. Some clearly saw Child

---

1 Bradshaw and Stimson (1997) have raised the question of the likely impact of payment directly into a bank account on the perception of Child Benefit as women's money.

Benefit as the only component in the househo
calculation which was for children, and remarked on
inadequate it was to provide for a child's needs. In practice,
Child Benefit was sometimes used to provide for children's
needs directly, often to buy nappies, and on clothing and
school-related expenses. In other cases, it was used as a
'lump sum' with which to pay bills.

WAGES

There were 19 households with wage-earners: 15 men and
four women. Wages were paid weekly into a bank account in
13 couples (over four out of five of the men in this study were
paid weekly, compared to just under two out of five men
nationally, New Earnings Survey, *Social Trends 27*, ONS,
1997). Only two couples had wages paid monthly into an
account, and four couples received wages weekly in cash.

- All the male wage-earners were from the Family Credit
  couples. All worked full-time except one and the mean
  wage was £132 a week (fewer than three in ten men
  nationally earned less than £250 a week in April 1996.
  Social Trends 27, ONS, 1997).
- Four of the six female wage-earners were from the Family
  Credit couples, and for two of these the claim for Family
  Credit was based upon their employment. The remaining
  two female earners were from couples in receipt of Income
  Support/Jobseeker's Allowance. None of the women
  worked full-time and their earnings ranged from £15 to
  £72 a week. They all earned less than £4 per hour, the
  average being £3.60 per hour (almost a quarter of all
  workers earn below £4 an hour. New Earnings Survey,
  Social Trends 27, ONS, 1997).

Perceptions of wages differed according to: the part they
played in the family budget, who earned them, and the
amount earned. Both partners saw wages as conferring on the
earner a greater entitlement to spend than on the non-earner,
even when in practice this entitlement was not used

individually by women. The notion of ownership of money being dependent upon earning is dealt with in more detail in Chapter 4.

Where *men's* wages were the main source of family income they were seen as an inadequate family wage, intended to keep a roof over the family's head, and to feed and clothe them. Beyond these essentials, wages provided such things as a family day out or a bit of fun, although often, as one man commented, 'we don't usually get to that point.' Wages were used for what was described as 'the main outlays' of mortgage, bills and food. In one case where the Family Credit was greater than the wage, the wage was seen as 'topping up' the Family Credit. Reference was made by both men and women to the fact that employers should be ashamed to pay such low wages, and some were awaiting with interest the outcome of the government's plans on a minimum wage.

Perceptions of *women's* wages depended on the amount earned.

- Where women's wages provided the main income, as for two couples, they were seen as providing 'the essentials', and also seen by both partners as conferring decision-making powers on the woman.
- One woman was working at two part-time jobs in addition to her partner's full-time job, and he anticipated being ineligible for Family Credit by the next renewal date. Her wages were seen by both as making a contribution to the financial 'pool', and were used as 'lump sums' for the payment of large bills. Another woman earning only the £15 allowed on Income Support was seen by herself and her partner, for whom she was a carer, as earning money to spend on herself socially; she kept this separately from the rest of the household income for this purpose, and was exceptional in doing so.
- Other female earners said they felt more entitled to spend on themselves from this source than from any other, although, as we shall see, they did not actually do so.

'ADDITIONAL' INCOME

Some *men* received income in addition to their regular wages or benefits, from regular or occasional overtime, tips, or 'cash in hand' payments for casual work. This 'additional' income was used either for collective or for individual purposes.

- Overtime, which was seen as supplementary wages, was spent on the family.
- Three men had jobs involving regular tips. None would disclose actual amounts, saying they were 'negligible', but all kept them as their own money for individual spending.
- Seven men reported occasional 'casual' earnings. They were usually between £10 and £15, but in one case the amount was £200. These earnings were regarded by both partners as the men's money to allocate. In four cases, both partners said this money was spent on bills or children's shoes and clothing. The £200 was spent by the man on his hobby. Two men kept their smaller amounts as supplements to their usual 'pocket money'.

Only two *women* had any 'additional' income, both in the form of 'lump sums'.

- One woman had received £100 inheritance, and another had received around £3,000 equity from a former marital home.
- Both women had jurisdiction over the allocation of this money, and both were planning to use the money for home improvements, although the recipient of the equity suspected that a substantial amount of it would have to be spent on car repairs.

The additional income received by these men and women belonged to the individual much more firmly than did benefit income or regular earnings.

FAMILY CREDIT

Family Credit is a tax-free cash benefit paid to employed and self-employed people with dependent children whose net family income is below a specified level. The amount received is determined by the number and ages of the children, and the family's total income and capital. It is awarded for six months, after which claims have to be renewed. In a two-parent family, it is formally the woman who applies. At the time of the research, the man was the main earner in just over three-quarters of all couples in receipt of Family Credit, and within that group the woman had no earnings in 93.5 per cent of cases (*Hansard*, 17 December 1997, col 241). In this study, the man was the main earner in all but two of the couples receiving Family Credit, and within this group the woman had no earnings in all but two couples. Couples in the study received Family Credit payments ranging from £5.51 to £74.94 a week. The average payment was £37.33 a week, compared to the national average of £57.85 for couples as well as lone parents (*Family Credit Quarterly Statistics*, May 1997, DSS).

Who claimed?

Women applied for Family Credit, and made the subsequent renewal applications. In one case, where the woman did not know how much her husband earned, and in another, where the man managed all the household finances, the men completed the form. Couples referred to the fact that the procedures and the forms dictate that the woman make the application in a two-parent family. Only one woman said that her partner was irritated that she was the recipient of Family Credit as the employee, at a time when her partner was unemployed, and that if he was employed and she was unemployed, she would still be the recipient. In addition, another interviewee commented that it seemed 'weird' that the woman received it when it was to boost his wages.

Nevertheless, it was clear that couples were able to 'make sense' of the fact that it is women who apply for Family Credit and, as we shall see in Chapter 7, this had considerable support. Some comments suggested that this method of payment was consistent with wider social expectations that women will apply for such benefits.

How Family Credit was held

- In a large majority of couples (13 out of 18 couples who had experience of Family Credit) the woman drew the money weekly by 'book' at the Post Office.
- In three cases, it was paid directly into a joint account, in one case into the wife's account, and in another the couple had changed from weekly to monthly claims as they adjusted from both being unemployed to a complicated 'box and cox' pattern of both being employed part-time.

Perceptions of Family Credit

Respondents made it clear that they would prefer not to have to claim any social security benefit at all, because of the stigma associated with being on benefits, the deprivation involved, and the inability to make progress and get on in life which being on a fixed low income entailed. With one exception, however, no stigma was felt to be associated with the receipt of Family Credit, and this may be because they felt fortunate to be in work:

> *I don't feel that it's degrading or anything like that. I mean, it's just one of those things, you know, it's 1997, there's a lot of people out of work. But I would personally sooner be working. I'd sooner feel as though I'm earning.* (Mr Bridges)

For some men Family Credit had acted as an incentive to work, as eligibility for Family Credit had been the crucial factor in their decision to take up employment. They saw Family Credit as a route to a better and more secure future with the kind of lifestyle others had, and although there was a feeling that they might be better off 'on the dole' financially in the short term, they did not want to take this option:

> *I was entitled to full rent rebate, full Council Tax rebate. I've got to be honest, we're better off unemployed, but it doesn't gi' ye nae incentive to live. I'd rather be, even if I were worse off, I would still rather be going out to work and make it worthwhile. I can't sit in the house all day, it's unreal... the job I've got now doesn't*

pay a lot. I mean, £76 doesn't go nowhere. If we didn't have the Family Credit it would, I think we would be out of this house. (Mr Cottam)

In two cases the payment of Family Credit had acted as an incentive for women's employment. For other women, their child-care responsibilities, rather than Family Credit, had acted as a disincentive to paid work.

Most men and women talked positively about Family Credit's contribution to the household budget. Some were pleasantly surprised at the level at which it had been assessed. Most men valued the function Family Credit performed in the management of the household finances, even though most of them were not directly responsible for this management. By contrast, most women valued it highly as a budgeting tool. A few men did talk of it as an unwelcome necessity, which should be replaced by an adequate minimum wage:

I think that your employer should be ashamed that you have to claim it, that they don't pay you a decent wage. The minimum wage, the government says that is the minimum you should earn and it's – it's annoying that you have to claim it anyway because they just don't pay you… I feel that the employer should pay you a decent wage for doing a job, you shouldn't have to go round with your cap in hand trying to get it just to pay the bills. (Mr Burrows)

A few women expressed a sensitivity to their partners' feelings when they alluded to their partners' dislike of claiming benefit because they were 'proud' men. They were angry on their partners' behalf that they had to work so hard, for such low wages, often doing 'unsocial' hours which had a negative impact on the family.

How Family Credit was used

Family Credit functioned in a number of different ways within the distribution of household income. It was seen by the majority of couples as 'her' money to administer because it was paid to women.

- Most women saw Family Credit as their 'own' money in more than an administrative sense. They had decision-making powers over its allocation, and this allocation was invariably to the family.
- Family Credit was typically spent on fresh food, nappies, school trips, and other needs of children such as clothing and occasional small toys. It was also combined with wages to pay regular bills such as rent and fuel.
- One woman for whom the Family Credit and the Child Benefit were her only source of income was very worried about possible plans she had heard of to 'do away with it'.
- In one case, where it was paid on the basis of the woman's earnings, it functioned in a similar way to a housekeeping allowance, but in a reversal of the usual direction it was given by the woman to her partner at home.
- In a few, less egalitarian households, Family Credit was 'appropriated' by the man: by being paid into an account to which the woman did not have access, or by being swallowed up on servicing male-incurred debts, so that the children became dependent upon extended family support for food. In one case, it lessened the call on the husband's wages, which were kept separately by him.

The *amount* of Family Credit received was also significant in its use:

- In families with just one child approaching the age of two, Family Credit of around £5 a week was spent on nappies.
- In a couple where it was around £70 compared to the man's earnings of £40, Family Credit was used to pay for rent and fuel in addition to nappies.
- In another family where the earnings were rising and the Family Credit reduced accordingly, the Family Credit was 'saved up' and used to pay the council tax bill.

INCOME SUPPORT/INCOME-RELATED JOBSEEKER'S ALLOWANCE

This is a means-tested benefit paid to those not in full-time work. Entitlement is based on the difference between income and requirements as measured by a set of scale rates and premiums. Half the couples in the sample were in receipt of Income Support/income-related Jobseeker's Allowance at the rates for couples, with children under the age of 11 years, plus family premiums. Rates at the time of interviewing were £77.15 for a couple, £16.90 for a child of under 11 years, and family premium of £10.80.[2]

Who claimed?

- Women claimed in only two cases out of the total number claiming Income Support/Jobseeker's Allowance. They were both claiming Income Support.
- For most couples receiving Income Support/Jobseeker's Allowance it was automatically assumed that the man would apply. The 'decision' was seen as a logical consequence of earlier work histories.
- Others engaged in strategic decision-making. Factors such as childcare, transport, educational issues, and advice from the Job Centre, particularly in the light of the change-over from Income Support to Jobseeker's Allowance, played a significant part in deciding who should claim. A number of couples had found it particularly confusing and difficult to negotiate their way through this decision-making process.
- The advent of the Jobseeker's Allowance reinforced the work patterns of those respondents who had traditionally nominated a male wage-earner. In addition, the apparent effect of stringently monitored and enforced legal requirements around 'actively seeking work' was to diminish the flexibility couples had to change their plans in response to the changing circumstances of child-care (their own inclinations and the availability of care for example), and

---

2   The first three couples were interviewed while 1996/97 rates were in operation.

employment plans and possibilities. Couples inclined or prepared to relax rigid demarcation of gender roles experienced pressure to 'solidify' a decision about which one of them would work and which be responsible for child-care, and this inhibited their ability to think in terms of responding flexibly to an increasingly 'flexible' job market. For couples who wanted to retain a stake in the employment market for whichever partner had the best prospect of success, the sharing of child-care associated with their efforts meant that they were in effect 'bending the rules' on actively seeking work. One man, seeking advice from the Job Centre on the route from Jobseeker's Allowance status to Family Credit eligibility via the building up of what he hoped would be his wife's 'small business', had been told that he should not be looking after their child during the day to allow her to attend meetings to promote her business.

How the Income Support/Jobseeker's Allowance was held and used

- In 10 out of the 15 IS/JSA couples, the man cashed the giro.
- Where the woman cashed the benefit, this was seen as appropriate by both partners because of her responsibility for managing household finances. Some men later cited this rationale when discussing alternative ways of paying benefit to families.
- In the two cases where the Income Support was in the woman's name, the woman usually cashed it herself, although one man sometimes cashed his disabled partner's IS for her.
- In 14 of the 15 couples, the money was then held as cash. In nine of these, the cash was simply handed over to the woman for her to manage. In four couples, men continued to hold and manage most of the cash.
- In two cases there was an element of segregation: one woman who both claimed and cashed the Income Support

gave half of it to her partner, and one of the three women in the study who did not know how much her partner received was given (an unspecified) part of the Jobseeker's Allowance which he had cashed.

- For most of the Income Support/Jobseeker's Allowance families, the only other source of income was the Child Benefit, so that the Income Support was the major budgeting resource for women.

Perceptions of Income Support/Jobseeker's Allowance

Perceptions of Income Support/Jobseeker's Allowance encompassed a number of different elements.

These benefits were frequently viewed as a subsistence income:

> *Enough money to survive on, but not enough money to live on.*

The change of name from Income Support to Jobseeker's Allowance also impacted on how it was viewed, sometimes eliciting scepticism:

> *They make me laugh the way they call it Jobseeker's Allowance, 'cos what do they think you're going to do with it? Take it in your pocket: 'I'll go and find a job with this.' I mean, it's a joke ain't it?* (Mr Scrimshaw)

The stigma attached to being reliant on benefit was also much in evidence with this benefit, unlike Family Credit. Women who had been lone parents, claiming in their own right, were particularly sensitive to this. Such feelings were reinforced by: negative comments from neighbours; what was felt to be 'degrading' treatment at Job Centres; and in some cases, being subject to investigation by the Benefits Agency.

A striking theme here was the extent to which recipients felt that they were dependent on *other people's* money, and that they had to be accountable in ways which employed people were not:

It's like a negative income, it's like er – [pause] – I guess the reality of it is that it's everybody that works and who pays taxes' money... sometimes I feel like I have to justify the money that I get and what I spend it on to the Benefits Agency... you're unemployed twenty four hours a day – whereas you may only be a builder for seven hours a day – whereas being unemployed is a constant thing, you're unemployed when you're asleep, it's not a nice thing to be. And it's like a label that someone's attached to you. (Mr Goodwin)

I don't feel I'm dependent on James – but dependent on the money the Government gives us, which I don't like – [Why?] I don't know, it's like nothing's yours – the house isn't yours, the money isn't really yours... because it's like taxpayers' money and... I feel guilty about it. (Ms Goodwin)

For another family, an attempt to see oneself and to be seen as a traditional family appeared to be a reaction to the imputed disapprobation:

Most people would say: 'Oh, it's money for nothing,' but it's not – we exist, and however guilty people might think we ought to feel, we don't. Robert paid 20 years' worth of National Insurance and we happen to be using it up now... it would be nice to be a traditional family, and I think we are – the only thing is that Robert doesn't happen to have a job at the moment. (Mrs Norton)

Some women saw it as their partner's money because it was paid to him in recognition of his job-seeking status. Whilst being aware that there is within it a component for them, the fact that it is spent on the family served to override this 'individual element' in practice:

I wouldn't get anything from the Child Benefit for myself, that's Julie's [daughter]. But the Jobseeker's – I'm not really sure because I know some of it is to cover for me, but it mostly goes towards the house so...? (Ms Parker)

Men too did not think in terms of individual components, but were more likely to see it as 'their' money with which to provide for the family:

> *I don't think half of it's hers and half of it's mine, I don't think of it like that. But in one way, I suppose I see it as mine to provide whatever.* (Mr Short)

FINANCIAL SUPPORT FROM FAMILY

- Almost without exception, couples received regular financial help from their extended family. Only the two oldest couples in the sample did not refer to such help.
- Support came most commonly from couples' own parents, in the form of cash, groceries, shoes and other clothing for children, and children's school trips. Adults often received clothing from family at birthdays and Christmas. Other help took the form of 'bailing out' at times of difficulty, by paying a bill related to the home or car, paying off arrears, or buying expensive 'white' goods or furniture.
- Many *women* reported fairly regular help from their own mothers. In the case of the most heavily indebted couple, the woman's mother sent her money on a weekly basis, and she was dependent upon this and the Family Credit with which to feed the family. A few *men* occasionally sought help with a bill or arrears from their own fathers – what one man described as 'having to go and give me dad a cuddle'. One man who had done so clearly saw the necessity as a 'failure' on his part.

SUMMARY

- The source, the amount and the recipient of household income were all significant for the ways in which it was perceived and allocated, with the amount being particularly significant for women's wages and Family Credit.
- In two-thirds of the couples, Child Benefit was cashed weekly by the woman. In the few cases where it was paid

into a bank account, this did not diminish women's access to it.

- Child Benefit was perceived as a benefit paid to women and earmarked for children. Its allocation was on children, either directly or via collective household expenditure.
- Men and women saw wages as conferring on the earner a greater entitlement to spend than on the non-earner, even when in practice this entitlement was not used individually by women.
- The allocation of 'additional' income differed according to its source and its recipient.
- Most couples receiving Family Credit accepted that the women claimed the benefit. Women spent it predominantly on the family. Family Credit was positively valued by men and women, despite a perception that it enabled employers to pay inadequate wages. Women particularly valued Family Credit highly as a weekly budgeting tool.
- Family Credit had specifically acted as an incentive to employment for some men and women. There was no clear evidence on whether Family Credit was acting as a disincentive to employment for women.
- Men in this study were able to separate Family Credit from the negative associations of out-of-work benefits. In a context of high unemployment, there was little evidence of a sense of stigma from claiming Family Credit.
- In the majority of cases, men both claimed and cashed the Income Support/Jobseeker's Allowance. This encouraged a perception for some men and women of this income as 'his money'.
- The changeover from Income Support to Jobseeker's Allowance appeared to reinforce the practice of men making the claim. Those who were trying to create a manageable shared pattern of combining caring for their family with paid employment were to some extent being inhibited from doing so because of a perceived requirement to identify conclusively which of them would be the wage-earner and which the child carer.

- The degree of stigma couples experienced as Income Support/Jobseeker's Alowance recipients was striking. As a consequence, some did not feel the money was theirs.
- There was a high incidence and degree of financial support from extended family.

Chapter 3

Patterns of financial management

This chapter explains how the allocation systems couples used were classified, and presents the patterns of financial management. Whilst allocation systems show how money in the household is managed, it is the ways in which *control* operates within them which reveal how they are related to inequalities in financial decision-making and in access to money. The chapter therefore goes on to discuss the concepts of management and control, and to illustrate how they were defined and used as analytical tools in our study. Finally, the way in which control is exercised at various stages in the process of financial management is discussed.

Using quantitative analysis of 1,211 couples from all socio-economic groups, Vogler and Pahl (1993) further developed Pahl's original Allocation Systems Classifications (see Chapter 1). In 61 per cent of the pooling households, at least one and often both partners saw one or the other of them as ultimately responsible for management. Vogler therefore broke down Pahl's original single pooled category into: male-managed, female-managed, and joint pool. She then used a seven-fold typology:

- female whole wage;
- male whole wage;
- female-managed pool;
- male-managed pool;

- joint pool;
- housekeeping allowance; and
- independent management.

She found that the most frequently used system was the female whole wage (26 per cent), while the system least used was the independent management system (2 per cent). For our group of low-income couples with children, we omitted the independent management system from the options offered interviewees because it was associated with dual earners. A detailed description of how and by whom the household income was managed was elicited from inter-viewees before they were asked to choose from statements characterising the classification systems. Couples' responses to the typology offered them made it clear, however, that a small number of them did, in fact, use an independent management system, and a few others incorporated some elements of independent management into their systems.

SOCIAL SECURITY INCOME AND INDEPENDENT MANAGEMENT

There were five couples in the sample whose arrangements did feature elements of independent management, demonstrating that this type of system is not used exclusively by dual-earner couples, as suggested by previous research. In some cases, elements of independent management rested on payment of a substantial amount of Family Credit to the woman, and this source of income made it difficult accurately to classify the management system according to the established typology. Since independent management was used by couples with separate sources of wage and benefit income coming into the household, it was a system associated with dual *income* as opposed to dual *earner* couples. In the other cases, independent management derived from an amount of Jobseeker's Allowance given to the woman by her partner, without her actually knowing the total amount he received. In these cases, a classification of housekeeping allowance was appropriate.

For two young couples who had only been living together since the birth of their two-year-old child, the evolution of their financial arrangements mirrored the development of their relationship, supporting Laurie and Rose's suggestion that 'independent management may exist in the early days of a relationship and be replaced by another form of organisation as relationships mature and couples enter into a longer term commitment to each other' (Laurie and Rose, 1994:231.

There were also a few women in female whole wage systems who appeared to be 'hedging their bets' on how far they could rely on their partners to limit their personal spending, by retaining sources of money which they had not disclosed to their partners. In addition, one couple who were classified as using a male managed pool had also built into their system an allocation to each of them of an equal amount of personal spending money, as a consciously egalitarian measure.

Classifying these couples highlighted a number of important points. It showed the way allocative systems can overlap. It also revealed the importance of the distinction between dual income and dual earner couples in classifying management systems. Finally, the association between payment of a substantial amount of Family Credit to the woman and independent management emphasised further the importance of the *source* and the *recipient* of income. The importance of income source has been suggested, for example in connection with budgeting period, and for higher income levels (Pahl, 1989) but not demonstrated by previous research (Hunt, 1980; Morris and Ruane, 1989).

The patterns of financial management for our couples are shown in Table 3.1. The table shows that almost two-thirds of the couples used a female managed system, with the female whole wage being the most frequently used overall. Of male-managed systems, a pooling system was the more common.

Table 3.1 Pahl's and Vogler's patterns of financial management

Segregated systems

Whole wage system
One partner manages all the household money except the other's personal spending money

Female whole wage	12
Male whole wage	1

'Housekeeping allowance'	3

One partner gives the other a housekeeping allowance; they then keep all the rest of the money, from which some bills may be paid

Pooling systems

Female-managed pool	8

All the money is pooled and finances are managed jointly, but the women has the major management responsibility

Male-managed pool	4

All the money is pooled and finances are managed jointly, but the man has the major management responsibility

Joint pool
Some money is pooled and some is kept separately; each has some management responsibility

Independent management	2

Finances are kept completely separate

Total	31

COUPLES' ALLOCATION SYSTEMS AND BENEFIT TYPE

Heavy reliance on state benefits and male unemployment were thought to be associated with the female whole wage system. Classifying the allocation systems by benefit type (Table 3.2) confirmed such an association.

Table 3.2   Couples's household allocation systems
by benefit type

| | | *Benefit type* | |
	FC	IS/JSA	Total
Allocation system			
Female whole wage	4	8	12
Male whole wage	1	0	1
'Housekeeping allowance'	1	2	3
Female-managed pool	7	1	8
Male-managed pool	1	3	4
Joint pool	0	1	1
Independent	2	0	2
Total	16	15	31

Couples on Income Support/Jobseeker's Allowance more
frequently used the segregated female whole wage system,
and couples on Family Credit the female-managed pool.
Vogler and Pahl (1993) demonstrated, however, that the effect
of male unemployment was mediated by the wife's employment status. In their study of all income groups, female *full-
time* employment was the key factor predicting the use of a
pooling system. In our study, none of the women was
employed full-time. Among the Income Support/Jobseeker's
Allowance couples, only one woman was employed, for five
hours a week. Among the Family Credit couples, however,
income paid to some women did form a substantial proportion
of the household income, and pooling systems were more
frequently used by Family Credit couples. The significance of
the wife's employment status in mediating the effects of male
unemployment for this study's specific category of low
income couples is dealt with in greater detail in Chapter 6.

CONCEPTUALISING MANAGEMENT AND CONTROL

Pahl's (1989) work emphasised two key distinctions, between
collective and *individual* expenditure, and between *control* and

management. The differences between collective and individual expenditure will be examined in the next chapter. Here we explain the way in which we classified patterns of management and control.

We defined power in a way which captured both the *contexts* and *dynamics* of control. We used couples' decision-making as part of our analysis, but conceptualised 'decision-making' as a process. We encouraged respondents to elaborate upon the processes through which certain expenditures had been initiated and executed. This approach moved away from the idea that the 'location' of control was typically associated with particular allocation systems, and viewed control as embedded in the interactions between partners. This uncovered, for example, the ways in which male control operated within female-managed systems.

We also viewed financial management as a process, with control being exercised at critical points along the path from money entering the household to it being allocated. In practice, an uneven distribution of resources and the benefits gained from these resources can occur not only when one individual gains greater access to the small amount of 'officially' uncommitted income, after allocation decisions have been executed, but before the point of having any 'left-over' income is reached. For instance, one partner may take or be given personal spending money, or may 'go without' more resources than the other in order to meet the commitments being prioritised at any one time. In addition, money may be accessed via a build-up of arrears on payments initially prioritised by the partner with financial management responsibility, or by 'bypassing the system' and undertaking expenditure using credit, which the other has responsibility for repaying. As we shall see, using credit in this way was an important factor in an unequal distribution of money within the household.

To explore the management/control paradigm in greater depth, and how it operated in practice, we used the information from interviews on couples' access to bank accounts, where applicable;[3] their decisions on such things as how and why their 'uncommitted income' was allocated; what happened to income from casual earnings; and how and why credit was used. We added to this, partners' responses to questions on how they related to each other on financial matters, and on this basis classified control as male, female or joint. This more complex conceptualisation of power within marriage/partnerships, allowed us also to develop a conceptualisation of family relations which encompassed both cooperating and conflicting elements, with a range of alternative strategies open to both partners, but some more satisfactory to one than to the other.

Control and allocation systems

The segregated whole wage systems were characterised by male control which was likely to be implicit. An agreed prior 'contract' between partners removed the need for further negotiation. There was a high level of consensus on the man's entitlement to a fixed amount of 'pocket money', even when he was not working. Where whole wage systems included personal spending money, which was regularly allocated to the man as his entitlement, both partners tended to report that there was no 'uncommitted' income over which to exert any control, and in such cases control was classified as male.

Conflict sometimes occurred in the segregated whole wage and housekeeping allowance systems when men spent more on themselves than the agreed amount, or when other factors tested and stretched the 'contract' so much that its underlying principles came to be questioned but not abandoned: for example, the prospect for a carer of her partner's accelerating physical deterioration, or a degree of stress over the financial situation that led to a period of depression for the woman. Here, a high level of stress had

---

3   Among Family Credit couples, 15 out of 16 used a bank account. Among Income Support/Jobseeker's Allowance couples, three out of 15 did so: one in order to pay the mortgage; one to pay the Housing Benefit cheque into; and one for repayment of a loan.

made explicit a real or potential conflict of interests between partners which was nevertheless being 'managed'.

In non-segregated 'pooling' systems the patterns of personal spending and of 'going without' were less formalised and static. There was a 'jointness' supported by ideologies of 'sharing' which left room for ongoing negotiation and re-negotiation, unlike the whole wage system. There was little overt conflict, and partners adopted a 'bantering' style to monitor and check each other's adherence in practice to the shared ideology.

In some couples where male control was being exercised within a pooling system, there was an evident struggle between partners, and conflict became apparent. Whether overt or covert, conflict was evident in these couples' relationships around the ways in which men undermined or sabotaged their partner's attempts to control spending.

Where male control was exercised via male managed systems, there was unlikely to be overt conflict, but some of the women in these couples expressed more unhappiness than their male partners and described feelings of low self-esteem, revealing an underlying conflict of interest. Mr and Mrs Short, for example, agreed that Mr Short should manage most of the income and keep and allocate any 'left-over', necessitating his wife asking him for any personal spending needs:

[You were saying it ['left-over'] might be in your wallet?] *Yeah from when I've been out shopping, and then it probably would stay there until she needed, for example, womanly things that she – I'll say 'my wallet's there'... as I say, not a case of this is mine and that's hers, the money's there for both of us... I don't like asking for money, I don't know whether it's chauvinitis or not but I don't think it's right that I shouldn't have any money in my pocket. Not that I'm in the bookies or in the pub or spending it, it's just having it, as a resource.* (Mr Short)

[what sort of amount might be left over?] *To be honest I can't even tell you because I don't dare ask him... I never actually take any money off of him unless – He does all the shopping anyway. I never actually say 'can I have £5 for this, can I have £10 for that?'... if I need a haircut or anything like that I'll say 'I really do need my hair done next time we get our money, can we kind of squeeze that in?... I found that really hard not being independent... but you just have to make do somehow, don't you... the only luxury I suppose is Chris's tobacco, erm, I don't smoke luckily. The only things I need are feminine hygiene types of stuff, and sometimes it's been hard to find the money for that.* (Mrs Short)

SUMMARY

- The couples in this study were typical of low-income families in their extensive use of female-managed allocation systems. Almost two-thirds of them used a female-managed system, with the female whole wage being the most frequently used overall.

- The female whole wage was most frequently used by Income Support/Jobseeker's Allowance couples, whilst Family Credit couples most frequently used the female-managed pool. This confirms an association between reliance on benefit income and the female whole wage system.

- The occurrence of independent management systems illustrated the advisability of including this pattern in any further research with low-income families, especially where receipt of an in-work benefit serves to constitute a dual-income household.

- Taking account of the contexts and dynamics of control allowed incorporation of both co-operative and conflictual elements of control, with a range of alternative strategies open to both partners, some being more satisfactory to one than to the other. Recognising the way power is negotiated within marriage/partnerships illuminated how male control can operate within both female whole wage and female-managed pooling systems.

- Control operated at key stages in the process of financial management: the point at which money first enters the household; when decisions are made about the allocation system adopted; at the 'endpoint' of allocation by accessing uncommitted income; and within management practices by influencing the prioritising of spending in ways which support or subvert individuals' practices.

Chapter 4

Individual and collective expenditure

In this chapter, we assess the merits of the distinction between *individual* and *collective* expenditure, as used in earlier research, as a way of determining who benefits from expenditure. Who the beneficiaries are within the different allocation systems, in both material and psychological terms, is dealt with in Chapter 5. Here, the usefulness of the concepts is discussed, as well as the meanings they have for the couples themselves. Illustrations are given of the way in which credit and debt may also be incorporated within the individual/collective paradigm. Couples' spending priorities and experiences of 'going without' are examined, as a way of illuminating the balance between individual and collective expenditure, and consideration is given to how these relate to allocation systems. The significance of the level of income available for who controls and benefits from it, is also addressed. Finally, individuals' evaluations of having 'money in one's own right' are shown to be part of the process through which partners access individual spending money.

A high proportion of household income was already allocated for couples receiving social security benefits, sometimes directly at source, to housing and fuel costs. The amount of uncommitted income available, after disclosed credit and debt commitments had been met, but before food expenditure, was examined. Using a fairly crude calculation, this indicated that the difference at this point between Income Support/Jobseeker's Allowance couples, and couples on Family Credit was in fact negligible. The patterns of intra-household distribution of financial resources within the allocation systems could not account for the level of un-committed income as calculated, although low income *per se* may account for the prevalence of female-managed systems.

Couples receiving Income Support/Jobseeker's Allowance normally get their housing costs met in full (via Housing Benefit), while those on Family Credit rarely do. Most of the Family Credit couples had mortgages and received no Housing Benefit. The income level comparison we made between IS/JSA and FC couples did, however, treat credit and debt as 'committed' income, and, as Chapter 3 indicated, an uneven distribution can result from the execution of control before this 'endpoint' of uncommitted income is arrived at, because control may result in personal spending on credit leading to debt. The proximity of the figures for the two benefit groups served to highlight, therefore, the potential significance, for the distribution of household income, of who incurs debt and for what purpose, and this is examined as part of the patterns of individual and collective expenditure.

'GOING WITHOUT'

Part of women's responsibility for managing the household income was the need to prioritise and re-prioritise spending. When women and men were asked about responsibility for ensuring that the children's material needs were met, both said that this was the women's domain. It was often the case that women took the main responsibility for vigilant restraint over both their own and their partners' spending in order to prioritise the children's needs first and foremost. Women's accounts of 'going without' were remarkably consistent with findings from earlier research (eg Middleton *et al,* 1997). They were much more explicit than the men about going without themselves in order to put their children first:

Oh, I've never put myself first, I've always put my children first, I always have done… I haven't been able to buy myself a pair of tights sometimes… I've always put my family first before myself – I think I take after my mum for that… Yeah, always put my husband and children first before myself. (Mrs Stirland)

I don't really buy nothing, you know. I'd spend more on the kids and make sure the kids are all right first… me oldest lad, he's into like Reebok and – he won't just wear – it's got to have a name on it. (Mrs Hoyle)

Some men shared their partners' prioritising of their children's needs. Fathers of school-aged children particularly talked about wanting to provide their children with the things other children had, such as school trips:

I've been on school trips myself, you know, I wouldn't want him having less than other kids and getting, you know, ridiculed or whatever, 'cause school can be quite vicious, so um, yeah he had to have it as far as I was concerned. (Mr Hawley)

The fact that women primarily managed the money, and took responsibility for ensuring that the children's needs were met meant, however, that men did not need to consider their own prioritising of spending. When men were asked in interview to do so, they tended to refer to this being part of their partner's remit. Men found it more difficult than women to give examples of 'going without' on a personal basis, other than on clothing. They often invoked their partner's attempts to curb their spending:

If we're going through a hard patch, she'll say, 'Do you really need to go and buy a newspaper?' and that sort of thing you know? Because I've always done it and I like to read the paper, I say, 'Well yeah I do'… If you ain't got the money you can't. You know, I don't go and buy things just for the sake of it. [pause] Well I suppose I do, one or two things. But I – [Like what?]… Well, like newspapers! (Mr Bridges)

Some men's personal spending was not apparent to their wives. In contrast to her husband, who in fact bought himself a cooked meal every day at work, Mrs Thackeray described them both as 'making do' with beans on toast, or eating 'as and when':

> *We make do with baked beans or whatever's in the freezer, just make odd meals. We usually, myself and my husband, just have one meal a day – 'cos we don't usually eat much in the day. And the kids, we just make sure they have what they need, and we just have as and when.* (Mrs Thackeray)

Where couples had substantial debts, meeting those commitments took priority over all else in order to avoid court action or re-possession, and women in these couples reported going without food and basic toiletries:

> *First of all the Alliance & Leicester* [loan] *and the TV licence... if we didn't pay it we'd get arrested for having a television... things that would affect the fact that if we got sent to prison or something, Thomas* [son] *would get taken into care. You don't want to affect your family in any way like that... then after that it's Thomas and then food... I'd tend to say 'Well OK, you have that – I'm all right, honestly', you know, 'I'm fine – don't worry about me, I'll have a toothbrush next time, when we've got the money...* (Mrs Norton)

There was also a gender dimension to the way going without certain goods was *experienced*. Both men and women talked of rarely buying new clothes, but women were more likely than men to experience this as a deprivation. Men were more likely than women to cite not going out for a drink with friends as a loss. Women tended to see staying at home in the evenings as less of a deprivation for themselves than for their partners. When both women and men did go out for a drink with friends (rarely together because of the costs of baby-sitting) cultural patterns meant that it was likely to be a less expensive occasion for women than for men.

PERSONAL SPENDING MONEY

In addition to 'going without' in order to prioritise the children's needs, income was unevenly distributed where one partner had a disproportionate amount of personal spending. At these income levels, personal spending by one partner automatically meant the other one 'going without'. With whole wage systems particularly, the 'pocket money' given to (or taken by) the 'non-managing' partner meant one partner was 'privileged' over the other. Whole wage systems often involved the man either getting a regular amount of pocket money, or regularly receiving such things as cigarettes, tobacco and cans of beer. This 'earmarked' spending money was clearly 'individual'.

In pooling systems, where control was more 'fluid', access to personal spending required justification. In practice, this justification involved recourse to a rhetoric of collective expenditure which revealed that respondents' own conceptualisations of the distinction between 'individual' and 'collective' were often located within traditional divisions of labour. Men tended to describe as 'silly' women's spending on small items to enhance the home, and they gave this, and women's spending on children's clothes, as examples of her 'personal spending' because it gave her pleasure:

> *I probably smoke ten cigarettes a day, alright, I have a cooked breakfast at work, okay... And I, that's why I say, I don't feel resentful if Mo goes out and spends £8 on the kids... maybe somebody says, well if you took a packed lunch you could save £25 a week. Yeah alright I could do... then, why should I? I don't go to a pub and spend £20 a night. So I deserve to keep what I've got... I'm trying to think of an example* [of partner's personal spending], *it's not easy 'cos she doesn't make many mistakes like that... sometimes if she sees a nice little outfit and I think crikey, that's a hefty price, I might have a go at her about it... but then I know she has to have her certain amount of pleasures in life and she loves seeing the kids dressed nicely.* (Mr Morris)

Mr Barlow articulated particularly well the way that the conceptualisation of spending as individual or collective was related to gender roles, as well as consumption itself being gendered:

> *It's like when you're going out and you buy buggies and all that, you can spend 500 quid on your buggies and your plastics and you think like, Christ, you could have had a car now. That's the way I look at it but I'm a lad… a lass might think 'Eee, I've got a lovely buggy'. I think a lot of women are more for their houses, lads might be more for their beer or their cars or their motorbikes, which is only natural.* (Mr Barlow)

Among couples, in addition to men's spending on newspapers and magazines, expenditure on cars was a typical area of conflict. Women put a low priority on this, while men saw such expenditure as fulfilling their 'collective' responsibilities because it was related to maintaining their identity in the labour market. The burden of passing the time for unemployed men also led to expenditure by them which had a dual function of individual leisure and contributing towards the family collectivity. Expenditure by several men engaged in DIY on the home fell into this category.

CREDIT AND DEBT AS INDIVIDUAL OR COLLECTIVE EXPENDITURE

Spending on credit and accruing debt can also be conceptualised as either individual or collective. Around a third of the couples said they had no outstanding credit commitments at the time of interview, and seven of these said they had no arrears either. Among the remaining couples, the range of arrears included £42 for one missed council tax payment or gas bill, £100 for missed rent payments, £200 for a missed mortgage payment, £400 electricity arrears, rent arrears of £900, and £1,000 water rates arrears. There was no clear evidence that arrears had resulted directly from one partner's individual spending, as normally they related to a household bill. The same could not be said for spending on credit.

The type of credit used differed depending on couples' source of income. Income Support/Jobseeker's Allowance couples typically used catalogues, the Social Fund, and 'loan sharks', while Family Credit couples used credit and debit cards, storecards, and bank and building society loans. At least two men had previously been declared bankrupt and others had defaulted on credit payments, and so had forfeited their eligibility for credit. In addition, two men who had become ineligible for credit regained access to credit facilities via their partners.

We distinguished between who undertook expenditure on credit and who were the beneficiaries of such expenditure. Some spending on credit was jointly undertaken on items for the home and children and, even though it may have been in one partner's name, this was classified as collective expenditure. In two couples, partners shopped jointly on credit for 'personal' consumer goods for each of them at Christmas, when they decided to 'reward' themselves for a preceding period of restraint. This was classified as individual expenditure.

In a small but significant number of couples, men engaged in spending on credit primarily to their own benefit, without their partner's prior knowledge or without their wholehearted support. These men used a 'collective' rhetoric to support their spending, but their partners defined it as individual 'leisure' spending. For example, one man spent hundreds of pounds on books and CDs, which he justified in terms of creating a congenial home environment. Two men had bought expensive computers and accessories. One justified it in terms of enhancing career prospects, the other by suggesting that the electronic keyboard attached to the computer was something his 23-month-old child could play with. Their partners viewed these purchases as the men's 'toys' :

He has a computer and he will buy things for that and justify. I mean, we play with it and it's a toy – but he will buy it and say 'Oh well, Craig can use it' – 'Don't be silly, no he can't!' But that's his justification. [And when you say you play with it, whose, what?] *Oh, it's his, Sean's* [husband] *bless him. He's very much into music and he links keyboards to the computer and plays. And I mean, Craig* [son] *does play with it.* [pause] *To a degree, I suppose.* (Mrs Ripley)

Spending, therefore, both directly and on credit, was 'gendered' both in terms of the particular items purchased, and in the way in which the categories of individual and collective expenditure were conceptualised and justified by those engaged in the spending. In this way, men located their spending on cars, for accessories as well as maintenance, within the context of their work identity and they therefore classified it as 'collective' expenditure, while a woman's spending on children was seen by both men and women as part of her personal identity, and thus regarded as for her 'individual' benefit. This highlights the difficulties, encountered in earlier studies, associated with making a straightforward distinction between individual and collective expenditure, especially in relation to the gendered nature of 'work' and 'leisure'.

OWNERSHIP AND ENTITLEMENT TO PERSONAL SPENDING MONEY

In addition to the rhetoric of collective expenditure, men also justified spending on themselves by recourse to the notion of 'entitlement' (see Chapter 2). Their earnings gave them this entitlement, a perspective shared by many of the women:

Everything's coming off my wages, so you feel well it's more mine than yours... when it's your money paying for everything you feel you've got more say in what should be. (Mr Burrows)

If I'd done all the work I'd say 'Oh well I want a little bit for myself for the doing of it'... if I've done some graft she'll say like 'It's your money, you've earned it, you do what you want with it' type of thing. (Mr Barlow)

Each partner was asked whether it was important to them to have money of their own, and in answering they automatically equated one's 'own' money with money they had earned themselves. Some men, both wage-earners and those in receipt of Income Support/Jobseeker's Allowance, answered that it would be 'nice' to have money of their own, but that it was not possible at their income level to do so, and still meet their children's needs. Men who had 'earmarked' pocket money were able to hold a view of prioritising the family, at the same time as 'owning' a small amount of the household income individually, by virtue of the formalised but taken-for-granted inclusion within the management system itself of this 'pocket money'. The fact that it was an institutionalised arrangement made their personal spending unproblematic for them. For a few men without a regular amount of pocket money, the legitimacy of having one's requirements anticipated and met was so taken for granted as not to seem incongruous alongside a 'collective discourse' of 'money for the family':

> *No – it's important to have money for the family. After all, when you get married you take on a commitment for life and thereafter you strive to ensure that that family is self-sufficient or as sufficient as you can make it. In my family, my wife knows what my likes are so she allows me to spend X, Y and Z on different things that I want.* (Mr Holland)

For some men, therefore, their income was at one and the same time collectively *and* individually owned. By contrast, for some women, making sense of the term 'own money' often necessitated referring back to when they had been wage-earners before the birth of their children. Others looked to the future, and saw the possibility of earning as a route to some independence within the family:

> *Something that's just mine you know, a little corner of my life that's mine, because nothing else is, everything's theirs and his, and I'd just like to have something that's mine and I can do what I want with.* (Mrs Rickards)

Most women did not have paid work. Despite a discourse of joint or shared money, spending their partner's wages on themselves, when they were not earning, was very difficult for women. Neither did the few employed women feel they 'owned' their wages, unlike men. In theory, women's wages were conceptualised as 'theirs', and as conferring decision-making powers. However, because they prioritised children's needs so highly, they were seen in practice as totally subsumed within the collectivity of the family. The equation of earned money and ownership and entitlement was therefore enacted differently by men and women. And for those women whose family life was constrained by an income derived solely from benefit, the question of 'own' money was one which did not 'actually come up':

> *I have some mad thoughts sometimes: 'Oh, I could just go mad and spend all this on myself'* [If you could, what would you spend it on, do you think?] *Well that's a good question, I wouldn't know... It's a long time since I had money of my own really, so –* [hesitation] *I'm just happy that I've got that bit of money to provide for my family, buy food.* (Mrs Stirland)

> *Because we have so little of it it's all just ours anyway – if we had enough left over at the end of the week to start thinking 'Oh, what can we do with this?' then I'd probably think 'oh, it'd be nice to have my own money'... but quite often the question doesn't actually come up.* (Mrs Norton)

Entitlement to spend money was strongly related to who earned it. This raises the interesting question of how couples wholly reliant on social security benefits viewed their income, which was not 'earned' by either of them. Although women perceived different sources of money differently, their prioritising of the children often precluded individual spending from *any* source. Over and above this, however, Income Support/Jobseeker's Allowance was seen to be 'officially' defined as collectively owned. Mr Burrows explained a view some other men and women also expressed, that since the purpose of Income Support/Jobseeker's

Allowance is to meet the needs of the family, and at a minimum level, no one has an entitlement within it to individual
spending:

> *Well no, because none of you've earned it. It's all claimed*
> *through the family basically. 'Cause benefit covers the minimum*
> *amount, whether it's written up in my name or in my wife's*
> *name, doesn't matter, we've claimed it for the family. You're not*
> *claiming just for you so you can spend it.* (Mr Burrows)

In other words, with this conceptualisation of benefit, the
income was *exclusively* 'collective'. Finally, as suggested in
Chapter 2, there was evidence that for some on Income
Support/Jobseeker's Allowance, their money was not even
seen as legitimately 'theirs', but as belonging to those in
work, who pay taxes. This served to create the feeling that
even their family was not 'entitled' to this money.

Ownership of, and entitlement to, money as a resource
was therefore defined in relation to its source. Whether
money was earned, and by whom, served to confer individual
or collective ownership. Men and women, however, operated
these equations differently in practice. Couples reliant wholly
on benefit may see this as money they are not actually entitled to at all, or as money which by definition is collectively
owned. The way these concepts operated played a part in
enabling some individuals to gain access personally to part of
the household income, whilst constraining others from doing
so.

Taking into account the 'dual' functions of individual and
collective benefit derived from some kinds of expenditure,
and the couples' own perceptions of these categories, we
identified spending which was collective and spending which
advantaged one partner at the expense of the other. In this
way, it was possible to assess relative deprivation within the
patterns of income distribution in the households. Examining
these patterns revealed distinct groups within the sample,
and these findings are presented in Chapter 5.

SUMMARY

- Women typically took the main responsibility for vigilant restraint over both their own and their partners spending in order to prioritise the children's needs.
- Men were less able than women to give specific examples of 'going without' personally.
- Most female whole wage systems incorporated a regular amount of personal spending money for the man.
- Couples' conceptualisations of the distinction between individual and collective expenditure were often located within traditional divisions of labour, in a way which legitimated men's personal spending and defined women's collective expenditure, for example on children, as personal.
- Different sources of credit were used by Income Support/ Jobseeker's Allowance and Family Credit couples.
- The distinction between individual and collective expenditure was also applied to analysing debt and expenditure on credit, in relation to their instigation and who benefited from these expenditures. Credit was a route to personal spending for some men, to women's disadvantage.
- The burden of time for some unemployed men led to spending by them on activities such as DIY and car maintenance, which had a dual definition of individual and collective expenditure. In this respect, the spending of money was related to the spending of time.
- There were gender differences in couples' spending, including on credit. These differences applied not only to particular items of expenditure, but to the way men and women saw their spending as being for either individual or collective benefit.
- For some men, their earned income was at one and the same time collectively and individually owned. Women's prioritising of the family meant that women's earnings did not incorporate a 'personal spending' component in practice.

- Income Support/Jobseeker's Allowance was subject to a 'multiple' definition of ownership, being seen as conferring on the man entitlement to spend by virtue of being the recipient; as collectively owned by the family with no personal spending component for any individual; and as rightfully belonging to tax-paying wage-earners rather than to the couples who received it.

Chapter 5

Who benefits?

Assessing levels of 'going without' and of personal and collective expenditure as described in Chapter 4 enabled the identification of three distinct groups of couples within the sample, with different patterns of material well-being:

- In an 'egalitarian' group of 12 couples, the distribution between partners both of deprivation and of individual expenditure appeared balanced.
- A 'traditional' group of 14 couples was characterised by the man (in all but one case) gaining more than his partner in terms of individual benefits, in relatively 'modest' but real ways.
- A 'male-dominated' group contained five couples where the man appeared to be the individual beneficiary to a significantly greater degree than the woman.

The question of psychological well-being and its distribution across the three groups was also addressed. This chapter first describes the three groups, and then examines the psychological well-being of the men and women within them.

WHO BENEFITS? PATTERNS OF FINANCIAL DISTRIBUTION AND MATERIAL WELL-BEING

Group 1 Egalitarian

The egalitarian group was predominantly female-managed. Responsibility for financial management was vested in one person, but both partners took responsibility for exercising self-restraint. Purchasing on credit, either from commercial or informal sources, was jointly undertaken to benefit the children and the home.

There was no pattern of regular earmarked personal spending for the man. Small amounts of individual spending were equally balanced between partners, for example, a night out where each spent about the same amount of money, or one partner's occasional magazine balanced by the other's occasional bar of chocolate:

> *The only money for myself is from the Family Credit if I want a bar of chocolate or something... No, he doesn't have any. Very cruel aren't I? Sounds really mean... He has his pint of milk a day as well, he takes his 32p to get a pint of milk round the shop... if we've stopped for petrol and I'm with him, he goes, 'Can I have some sweets?' or 'Can I have a magazine?' and I don't like to say no.* (Mrs Clark)

> *He likes body-building and he supports Liverpool – just sort of something for himself, I suppose, 'cos he does, month in, month out, he never really has – mind you, I don't have anything for myself either. But I do go to aerobics every week and he goes body-building, you know, weight training. And I wouldn't not do that 'cos I think I'd climb the walls if I didn't have that.* (Mrs Bridges)

Maintaining such a balance entailed a degree of mutual monitoring and chiding. Both partners shared the same financial priorities, an equal commitment to the children both in theory and in practice, and a norm of shared deprivations, and occasional small purchases. One couple articulated this balanced approach particularly well as they described a recent change in their circumstances. Mr and Mrs Cottam had rent arrears of £900 and private loans for furniture and children's clothing totalling around £2,500. Mrs Cottam had been looking after the home since the children were born, and Mr Cottam had had a four year period of unemployment. Recently they had become a dual-earner family, both working part-time and claiming Family Credit. Mr Cottam attributed his success in the labour market to presentational skills learned at the Job Club. This had boosted his self-confidence in a number of areas, including financial management. Mrs Cottam's employment meant that she could no longer undertake sole management of the household income, and both she and her husband recognised that they could share this role, and were experimenting with ways of doing so.

Mr and Mrs Cottam struggled with both their serious financial situation, and complicated domestic arrangements arising out of their work lives. The car, which was essential to this, remained a heavy drain on their income. Mr Cottam bought parts from the scrap yard to keep it on the road. Neither spent on themselves and, as with other couples in this group, there was a strong theme of sharing the struggles and the deprivations. This originated for them from both starting paid work. The consequent change in management responsibilities and in the balance of control, initiated by Mrs Cottam, had required a shift on both their parts, as she explained:

> *Neil thought he hasn't got the brains to work things out. He's not very good at maths so it's always been left up to me, and now when I got sick of it he sort of had to do it. Now he knows he can, it's not the matter of having the brains or anything. I think most of it was my fault as well 'cos I always went – just took it as always me, so I just did it, but then I'd had enough.*

There was a large measure of common ground in the contents of the accounts given separately by couples in this group, and a high degree of consensus on their feelings and attitudes about their financial lives. On the whole, they felt they were making ends meet, but whether they were just stable and managing, struggling to keep afloat, or getting into heavy debt, there was a strong sense that they were in it together.

Group 2 Traditional

Both men and women in the traditional group 'went without' and experienced disadvantage. The women had no regular money to spend on themselves, however, while the men's need for some small *allocated* resources was maintained. Most often, this took the form of either actual pocket money (between £5 and £10 a week), cigarettes or tobacco, or a 'protected' night out with friends at the pub – expenditure which was not 'balanced' by any individual spending by their partners.

The men in these couples were not spending huge amounts of money and leaving their partners and children destitute. Nevertheless, as a proportion of a very limited income, their individual, privileged and regular access to a part of it was significant.

> *Darren goes out every now and again. Like, if there's a football match on, they go and watch it on Sky somewhere, something like that... If I go anywhere it's round my mum's or his mum's, it don't cost much and Julie likes to see her nan.* (Mrs Parker)

> *Where I go to sign on... there's a bus every two hours, a two hour wait for the bus to come back... so it costs me money to get there and then it costs me money sometimes to go for a pint just to kill the time to get back on the bus.* (Mr Short)

> *When I get the dole now, say I get £10 to last us a fortnight, that's my pocket money like, £5 a week. It might not seem a lot but I don't really need much. I'm used to what I get type of thing.* (Mr Barron)

The men in this group rarely questioned their wives' spending. They valued her skills, appreciated that she was undertaking a difficult job which they did not want themselves, and knew that she did not usually spend unwisely. They felt that they too were making sacrifices in 'only' having the small amount of pocket money, the tobacco, the 'last' pint. Their partners' lack of individual spending was not apparent to them. As we have seen, spending on the children was interpreted by some men as women's 'personal' spending.

There was one couple in this group where the wife appeared to benefit more. Mr Burrows was angry that he had little or no access to the household income. He usually lost the arguments which ensued when he tried to negotiate access. The ideologies underpinning the allocation of household income were very explicit in the arguments between Mr and Mrs Burrows, with claims and counter-claims for individual entitlement revolving around being the wage-earner on the one hand, and being the money manager on the other. Mr Burrows lost out both ways. He conceded to his wife's argument that he had no claim on the basis of management since this was wholly her responsibility, and no claim on the basis of wage-earner as this was something he was seen to be doing very inadequately.

Mr and Mrs Burrows used a segregated system, and each had suggested at times their partner undertake the other's role, but in practice neither wanted to: Mr Burrows did not want to have to do the managing, and Mrs Burrows did not want to do any paid work outside the home. Mr Burrows never questioned his wife's personal spending on clothing but Mrs Burrows required him to justify his spending to her:

> *If I went out and bought something, he wouldn't say, 'Where's the money for that come from?' It's 'Oh, that's nice' and he wouldn't really question it because he doesn't really know how things are.* [What about the other way around?] *Yes.* [pause] *I hadn't really thought about that till now. Yes, if he went out and bought something, I'd say 'Where the hell's the money for that gonna come from?'*

Mr Burrows was not actually given any money from the weekly housekeeping which his wife allocated herself from his wages. He was unaware both of the existence of one of a number of building society accounts she had opened, and of the actual amount in them. Her strict and highly organised budgeting meant that they were able to pay all the bills, improve the house, save towards a modest holiday, buy family birthday presents, and pay for the children to go to playgroup and dancing lessons. His only independent spending was when, much to her annoyance, he occasionally took a pound from his wife's purse to buy chocolate for himself.

Group 3 Male-dominated

In this group there were indications that the men were managing to access resources for themselves which were of some magnitude in the context of low household income. Two men were in occupations which traditionally attracted extra income in the form of tips, and they kept these as personal spending. Mr Ripley, who was a taxi driver, justified spending money on his computer and accessories to his wife. Mrs Ripley did not feel she had the right to spend on herself at all, but sometimes had to justify spending on their son, especially the price of shoes which he had just begun to wear.

Mr Dakin also received tips. He was initially hesitant in talking about personal spending, but after some reflection identified his passion for cars and car accessories, and his smoking, as items of personal expenditure undertaken from his tips.

Mr and Mrs Norton had initially spent jointly on credit on items for the house. They were offered through the post a credit card, just before Christmas, and used it to buy presents and DIY materials. They took out a loan of £2,500 at Mr Norton's suggestion, to pay off the credit card purchases, but then used the card for more spending on DIY materials. Mrs Norton had also been given money by her mother, which had been set aside for when she got married. This was spent on a computer for her husband. He then got connected to the Internet, the use of which had resulted in arrears with the telephone bill. As far as justifying spending to each other was concerned, Mrs Norton said:

> *We both do it... if it's Robert's, something for him, he usually says to me 'Is it all right?' It generally is, but it's nice that he says. And if I ask him, I'll say 'Well?' and he'll either say 'Well, we haven't got that much money', and I'll say 'Don't worry about*

*it then,' and I'll try and be all bright and breezy, but inside feel
awfully disappointed that we can't have silly things, and
sometimes you're brought up short like a choke chain.* (Mrs
Norton)

Mr and Mrs Holland also had outstanding credit bills for
purchases made on the prospect of Mr Holland starting a job
which did not in fact materialise. Some of this spending was
on family Christmas presents, but what Mrs Holland described
as 'a good half' was in connection with Mr Holland's hobbies.
Mrs Holland's only 'individual' activity was a night class in
book-keeping, which was free as a Family Credit recipient.
She thought her husband enjoyed being able to undertake
personal spending more than she did, explaining:

*He loves his books and classical CDs and I don't mind him
spending on that rather than spending on you know, night after
night down at the local pub.* (Mrs Holland)

Mr Holland gave a detailed account of a very checkered work
history, and a history of debt. A total of around £9,000 had
been repaid over about an 8-year period. His full social life
entailed a high degree of personal spending. When unemployed, he relied on his expenses as a councillor for this. In
addition, his wife had provided him with money to supplement
a £200 payment he received for casual work, to spend at a
model railway fair. He also asked her for money to buy wine,
and he echoed her view that she found this preferable to him
propping up a bar somewhere. He had recently conceded to
his wife's plan to sell the car, and because he was still
spending £80–90 a month on his bookshop storecard, she had
destroyed the card. He described his large collection of books
and CDs as part of the home environment he had created:

*As far as I'm concerned, they lend themselves to the environment
that I've created for myself. But not as much as my wife is to it,
and our daughter. So I'm – given the choice between a
locomotive and my wife, I know what I'd choose, but I'm not
gonna say what it is!* [laughs] *Of course, it's my wife! You can
only watch a locomotive go round a circular track so many times*

> *and then you get bored with it. My wife can do many, many*
> *things.* (Mr Holland)

He did recognise that one of the things she could do was to manage the money, quite cheerfully admitting that he was hopeless at this.

Mr Thackeray also had a history of debt. He explained that his first wife had made him pay his wages into her own account before the marriage broke down. When he met his current wife, he had his own bank account again, but soon exceeded his overdraft limit, and had his cheque book and cheque card withdrawn. As soon as his wife was 18 years old, therefore, he changed his account to a joint one, his wife took over the financial management, and he used her credit facilities. After a while, they discovered that he was able to get credit in his own right again. At the time of the interview, they had five separate storecard accounts, three credit cards spent up to their limits, three catalogue accounts, two of hers and one of his, and an overdraft of £800. Their total credit commitments stood at about £10,000, and they had got into spiralling debt. Mrs Thackeray met these commitments regularly, but then had to buy food on credit. In addition, her mother sent her money every week.

Mrs Thackeray felt she had got 'bogged down' in a vicious circle of debt. It had been undertaken jointly initially, but she now found it difficult to persuade her husband to stop and to recognise the seriousness of their situation:

> *I don't think he really realises the seriousness of our situation.*
> *You can tell him till you're blue in the face but it doesn't sink in,*
> *it just goes through one ear and out the other... I think he tends*
> *to avoid it. He doesn't like to admit 'Oh yeah,' you know, 'I've*
> *got to stop.'* (Mrs Thackeray)

Mr Thackeray was fully aware of the extent of their debts, but he had also just bought a computer for £1,300 for which they did not have to begin payment for another six months, and he was trying to persuade his wife to allow him to buy a digital camera to go with it:

Now I've got a computer upstairs, I'd like a scanner and a digital camera... sometimes when I'm looking through magazines and think 'Oh', you know, 'I'd really like that,' I have to virtually pinch myself to think, well, you've gotta think sensibly here... I try not to think about money when I can help it. (Mr Thackeray)

And he didn't see himself changing in the future:

I am atrocious with money. I always have been, and now I'm 30, I think I realise that I always will be. (Mr Thackeray)

In this group, therefore, men had access to money in addition to their wages, which they used for personal spending. Three men spent on themselves the tips they received, without disclosing the amounts to their wives. Three men used credit to buy expensive consumer goods, creating debts which women had responsibility for servicing. Women were disadvantaged in material terms and, as we shall see, also suffered in terms of psychological well-being.

WHO BENEFITS? PSYCHOLOGICAL WELL-BEING

Previous research suggested that responsibility for the management of household finances undertaken by women in low income families is likely to be a burden rather than a source of power (Wilson, 1987; Pahl, 1989; Vogler, 1994; Kempson, 1996). The men and women in our study were asked whether there were any individual advantages and disadvantages associated with their patterns of household management, and whether they worried about money generally.

In only two couples did *both* partners say that they did not worry or experience stress about money. In all the other couples interviewed, there was stress and worry. Findings were consistent with those of Bradshaw and Holmes (1989) in showing that men and women's experiences were associated with the specific roles each played in the financial organisation of living on a low income.

Women reported far higher levels of stress and worry than men. It was most acute when associated with debt, but women typically described stress related to: being unable to provide as well for the children as they would like; the constant, unremitting burden of having to prioritise and re-prioritise spending; the need to exercise vigilance and restraint not only over themselves but over their partners too; and the implicit accountability in having to reveal 'failure' to one's partner when it became impossible to make ends meet.

I hear them in the nursery... and I think, I wish I could do that for my bairns, but I can't 'cos I haven't got the money. (Mrs Barlow)

It takes a lot of guts to tell Tony that we're overdrawn... I feel very very guilty about it... 'cos I hold the money and I'm meant to be able to spend the money that we've got, and not money that we haven't got. (Mrs Macmillan)

Some nights I'd lie awake worrying about where are we going to get the money from for this? Neil went straight to sleep, had no worries or anything! [laughs] (Mrs Cottam)

Things are bad enough when they're normal but when things do get low, you just seem to be in a hole – when's things going to get better? when are we going to get a bit of money to do something as a family? (Mrs Rickards)

I feel jealous when I go to shops – you know when you see people and they've got trolleys piled high and I've just got things what's just covering bottom – it hurts. (Mrs Stirland)

Despite this, women also expressed the 'peace of mind' gained from undertaking financial management, and a sense of pride in the effective fulfilment of a difficult and onerous job. There was some evidence that women's 'peace of mind' and pride made it difficult for them to relinquish the role of financial manager despite its inherent stresses.

If it's all paid for, if all them bills are paid on time and I haven't got no red letters or people threatening to cut me off then that's peace of mind. If I've got food in my cupboards, it's peace of mind... obviously, I'm more proud when I've got something left from it, and I can say, oh look, you can have a new pair of – then you get smiles and things and it's nice. (Mrs Stanley)

Men often recognised both their partners' financial management skills, and the advantage they reaped by not having to worry as a result. In contrast to women being reduced to tears and having sleepless nights because of worry, men typically had a 'fatalistic' attitude, that creditors couldn't take what the family doesn't have:

I don't worry about nothing. No, life's too short to worry. If something's going to happen, it'll happen... they can't have money that I haven't got. (Mr Short)

Some women also worried less because of a partner's attitude, or past experiences of managing an inadequate income:

I just think if we ain't got it we ain't got it. If we haven't got it, no-one else can have it. I've found now, if you do get into difficulties with bills, if you phone the people up, then they'll always help you out. (Ms Morris)

The stress involved in managing a low income was also experienced by men with this responsibility. Conversely, their partners spoke of being relieved of this worry. Mr Bartram had both financial management and control, and his wife reported no worries at all:

[Do you worry about money?] No, because, sorry but he pays it. I feel sorry for him. I said like, 'What's up with you?' and he'll say, 'Well what we going to do?' I said 'If it works out, great.' As I said, something always works out. (Mrs Bartram)

More typically, men's stress and worry were associated with their perceived responsibility for securing, keeping, or making progress in employment. When women moved into the role of main wage-earner, they too began to worry about fulfilling this responsibility successfully, and less about the management of the household finances, responsibility for which had devolved to the male partner.

The fact that women carried responsibility for financial management across all three groups meant that the distribution of psychological well-being across the three groups favoured men overall. Those men who worried least or not at all were in the 'traditional' group. This was because they had little or no involvement in financial management, and had retained a small degree of financial autonomy through a regular amount of personal spending money. Having this money, however small the sum, was important:

> *I think I've getten a good 'un – when she gets the dole, she's got a book which she keeps her records in... I get my pocket money and that's it... I think I'd shout at her if she says 'Where's that fiver gone?' [laughs] No, don't have to justify where it's gone. I think if she was giving us a hundred quid a week pocket money, and I came in with a fiver, then I think she would be able to play hell with me.* (Mr Barlow)

The stress and worry experienced by men in the egalitarian group were predominantly related to being unemployed or to their status as low wage earners, except for two men in male-managed systems who displayed the same kinds of worries as the women who carried these responsibilities. One of these commented on the sense of security associated with management responsibility, in a similar way to women's references to 'peace of mind':

> *It's not from any incompetence on Claire's part at all... if I haven't got the money there, I don't feel secure... I don't feel right when Claire looks after the money – it's not because she can't do it, it's because I don't feel secure when I'm not looking after it.* (Mr Goodwin)

The disparity between men's and women's reported psychological well-being was most marked in the male-dominated group, where most of the women worried a great deal, particularly when there were debts which they had to manage. Overall, *responses* to stress also showed differences along gendered lines, with women being more 'expressive' of their stress and worry and men being more 'stoical' about theirs. Men also tended to express anger, and women to report depression and to become tearful in interview.

SUMMARY

- Couples divided into three distinct groups according to the balance of material benefit and disadvantage between the partners. An egalitarian group of 12 couples was predominantly female-managed in a pooling system, and couples shared material benefits and disadvantages. Expenditure by credit was jointly executed and for collective advantage. In a less evenly balanced group of 14 couples, most of whom used a female whole wage system, the man (and in one case the woman) were privileged in relatively modest but real ways, for example, in terms of cigarettes/tobacco, evenings out, cans of beer at home and magazines. In a small group of five couples, men were individual beneficiaries to a significantly greater degree than women, by spending on expensive items such as model railways and computers/computer accessories.

- Across all three groups, women reported higher levels than men of stress and worry about finances. It was most acute in relation to high levels of debt. Some women, whilst finding the management responsibility burdensome, also derived peace of mind and a sense of pride from their skills as managers of a low income.

- Men's accounts of stress and worry were more typically associated with their perceived responsibility for securing, keeping, or making progress in employment. The stress involved in financial management among low income families was experienced by men when they did have primary responsibility for it. Conversely, their partners spoke of being relieved of this worry.

- Responses to stress differed along gendered lines. Men more often expressed anger and women more often reported and exhibited feelings of depression.
- In the even or uneven distribution of both material and psychological benefits, men's personal spending was a significant factor, particularly where the use of credit and other 'new forms of money' effectively subverted women's financial management.

Chapter 6

Explaining patterns of distribution

Having identified couples' allocation systems and distribution patterns, and examined their material and psychological impact, we now turn to explanations for these patterns. We consider a number of possible explanatory factors in relation to patterns of financial distribution: the resource theory of power, which suggests that equality in household financial arrangements depends on equal positions in the labour market (Vogler and Pahl, 1993:79); the ways in which couples' evaluations of and participation in 'breadwinning' mediate the distribution of household income; and the role played by the couples' 'marital careers'. The three groups are examined with reference to these factors.

In explaining patterns of distribution, we develop further the typology of the three groups identified in the previous chapter. We examine each group's allocation systems, the benefits received, and their patterns of control. Evidence from previous research is used to guide investigation of the ways in which control related to egalitarian or inegalitarian distributions of income, and the implications of this are discussed in Chapter 8.

ALLOCATION SYSTEMS, BENEFIT TYPE, AND FINANCIAL
CONTROL

We look now at the patterns of allocation system and benefit
type across the three groups. Table 6.1 shows the groups'
allocation systems, and Table 6.2 shows the social security
benefit the groups received.

Table 6.1   The three groups' allocation systems

		Groups	
	Egalitarian	Traditional	Male- dominated
Allocation system			
Female whole wage	3	9	0
Male whole wage	0	1	0
'Housekeeping allowance'	1	2	0
Female-managed pool	5	1	2
Male-managed pool	2	0	2
Joint pool	1	0	0
Independent	0	1	1
Total	12	14	5

Table 6.2   The three groups by type of benefit

		Groups	
	Egalitarian	Traditional	Male- dominated
Benefit type			
Family Credit	9	4	4
Income Support/ Jobseeker's Allowance	3	10	1
Total	12	14	5

These tables show that:

- Those in the egalitarian group, where the benefits and deprivations were evenly distributed, were largely in receipt of Family Credit, and used pooling systems.
- Those in the traditional group, where men were 'modestly' privileged, were mostly Income Support/Jobseeker's Allowance couples. They used segregated systems: predominantly the female whole wage, but also the housekeeping allowance and the male whole wage.
- Those in the male-dominated group, where men enjoyed significant individual benefit, were mostly Family Credit couples, and used a mixture of male- and female-managed pools, and independent management.

Tables 6.1 and 6.2 show that source of income cannot totally explain the differential distribution of resources, as both the egalitarian and the male-dominated groups contained couples receiving Family Credit. The income of those in the traditional group, however, was more fixed than that of other couples. They had very little 'casual' paid work, no opportunities for overtime and fewer sources of credit. This more fixed level of income may have inhibited the degree of imbalance between couples within this group, regardless of their type of benefit.

As already suggested, the amount of 'uncommitted' income was very similar for both Family Credit and Income Support/Jobseeker's Allowance families. Consequently, income level was not a crucial factor where the income levels are uniformly low. The calculation of 'uncommitted' income did, however, treat credit and debt as 'committed' income, and, as Chapter 3 indicated, an uneven distribution can result from the execution of control before the 'endpoint' of uncommitted income is arrived at. Personal spending on credit was a significant example of this in the male-dominated group. The fact that most of this group were in receipt of in-work benefit meant they were able to use commercial forms of credit. What distinguished their credit spending, and the relative deprivation between partners, from those using credit in the egalitarian group, was once more a distinction between collective and individual expenditure.

It was primarily *individual* expenditure by men, whether directly, or on credit, which was responsible for an uneven distribution of income in the male-dominated group. If we now look at the distribution of control across the three groups, shown in Table 6.3, the operation of male control, which enabled men's access to individual spending, becomes clear.

Table 6.3   Control by group

	Female	*Control* Male	Joint
Group			
Egalitarian	2	0	10
Traditional	2	11	1
Male dominated	0	5	0

What were the factors which meant that female management, subject to joint control, translated into an even distribution of resources for those in the egalitarian group, and what factors led to male control being translated into female disadvantage in the traditional and the male-dominated groups?

CONSTRUCTIONS OF BREADWINNING

Vogler's (1994) analysis highlighted the importance of breadwinning responsibilities, and showed that who has, or is seen to have, ultimate responsibility for these is a more powerful factor than that of domestic divisions of labour *per se* in explaining allocation systems. What is unclear from her quantitative analysis is *how* 'breadwinning' might be related to control, and thereby determine material outcomes, especially for couples on social security. We now investigate this.

Pahl (1989) and Morris (1984) also drew attention to female participation in the labour market as a way of enhancing women's authority over decision-making. Vogler and Pahl (1993) suggested that women needed to work full-time for this to be the case. In contrast to their studies, all the households studied here had low incomes. What may be of greater significance in the current study is women's earnings as a *proportion* of the household income, and how this relates to breadwinning.

In drawing upon interviewees' responses to scenarios put to them of a family's main income being derived from wages paid wholly to men, wages paid wholly to women, or derived from a combination of men's and women's wages, we identify different models of breadwinning, which further develop the typology of the three groups described in Chapter 5. These three different models of breadwinning underpin the operation of control, shown to be crucial in egalitarian or inegalitarian distribution patterns. The models of bread-winning subscribed to by the three groups are now presented, and the factors associated with them examined.

The egalitarian group: adaptive breadwinning

Earlier research (Vogler, 1994) suggested that men's attitudes to their own and women's employment exert a more powerful influence on women's labour market participation than women's own attitudes to their employment, and that women are influenced by their partners' negative attitudes towards women's paid work (Thomson, 1995). We will see this exemplified in the traditional group. However, there was also evidence in our study of influence between partners in the opposite direction. In the egalitarian group, the men's desire to be the main breadwinner may have been modified by the employment opportunities open to both partners, and also by their partners' demands arising from their former financial experiences within marriage. Only a few women in this group were engaged in paid work, but both men and women conceived of breadwinning as a joint activity. Their pre-dominant use of pooling systems to manage the household income, and shared control in both male- and female-managed pools, were both compatible with this perspective.

All except two of the men in this group were their family's main breadwinner, but they did not all see this as the only acceptable option. Three women in this group were currently working, one had just had to give up work for lack of child-care, and another was pursuing a college course which they both hoped would lead to employment. Men in this group who had held 'traditional' views about breadwinning had been influenced by their own inability to find work paying a 'family wage' and their partner's ability to do so, either alone or in combination with them. Mr and Mrs Cottam, described in the last chapter, exemplified this. Mr Cottam had been claiming Jobseeker's Allowance, but the availability of Family Credit had served to facilitate his entrance into the labour market. He still felt strongly that he should be the 'sole provider', and he still saw his wife's earnings as a supplement to his own wages. His work was 'part-time', however, and was not therefore regarded as a 'family wage'. Since his wife became employed, she could no longer carry the whole burden of financial management. Together, these factors had functioned to 'equalise' their position. Labour market conditions had not served to change Mr Cottam's attitudes, but had served to alter his behaviour.

For two couples, their work and domestic organisation effectively constituted a 'role swap'. Mr Barber used to have a more senior position than his wife in the insurance firm where they both had worked. He was now more of the junior partner in his wife's burgeoning business. Long-time married and long-time owner-occupiers, they were not incurring many of the household expenses that many other families wholly reliant on social security continually face, associated with setting up home, or with moves precipitated by financial insecurity. Their interviews conveyed a real sense of 'jointness' and 'teamwork', which was being reinforced by their plans to go into business together.

Mr and Mrs Bridges had also considered a role swap but it would not have been economically viable because of transport costs:

My wife's said to me about me staying at home and her going to work 'cos sometimes she can earn more money than me. But then again, taking into account she would have to use the car [currently off the road] *it wouldn't really be a lot different anyway.* (Mr Bridges)

Mr and Mrs Smales were agreed on the desirability of the male breadwinner. Mr Smales wanted ideally to be the main earner from a sense of 'male pride'. His wife appreciated this. She also valued her own domestic and parenting role, but she recognised the power of external constraints:

I'm not saying that if you go out to work you're wrong, because you're not. Some situations it simply leaves the wife no choice – if the wages aren't good enough and the Family Credit don't help, some women just are left with no choice but to get a part-time job. (Mrs Smales)

Their consensus on traditional divisions of labour did not lead to an uneven distribution of resources. The significant factor appeared to be that Mrs Smales had been a separated lone parent before she and her second husband met, with control over her own income. As a result, she had insisted that he become free of the debts he had accrued as a single man before they moved in together:

Carol wouldn't let me move in with her full time until all my debts were paid off so that's what I did... when she asked me what my finances were and I... beat around the bush a bit. She goes 'Right, I don't want you coming in here with any debt. If you move in, we've got to start afresh, no debts.' (Mr Smales)

Mrs Smales' system in her first marriage had been the female whole wage. Once she had split up with her first husband, however, she had learned that she was fully capable of supporting her family herself:

When I was on my own with Patrick [son], *if that bill didn't get paid it was my fault. It was my responsibility to do it and I did it. And I managed quite well thank you very much. Because there was nobody else around to depend on. And that's probably why I am the way I am now.*

She graphically described the 'dynamics' of control in their marriage:

The children are the priority, and it is my job to make sure that they're all right. Nobody else is going to worry about it. It falls to me... he'll go along with it because he always does... I do like being in control, but... I want to give him the opportunity to say what he wants. But he knows what I want to hear him say and this is probably why he sits there and says, 'Whatever you like, it doesn't matter, you know me.' So he can't win, poor thing.

Mrs Williams also had more control of the income than in her first marriage. She now worked part-time and claimed Family Credit whilst her husband stayed at home. She compared their 'reverse housekeeping allowance' system with arrangements in her first marriage:

Everything were his and he just gave me some, even though we were both working... I think it makes you aware of, if you're in a relationship, things should be equal. Nobody's better than anybody else whether it's financially or anything else, that's why we are as we are... we learn through experience, don't we?... when I met Stuart we both had pasts and we talked about it... if you make a decision that a relationship's equal on all terms, not just financial... we made that decision, and it's worked for us. (Mrs Williams)

Mrs Bridges had also 'come out of' a first marriage; she felt she had been financially better off as a lone parent,[4] and was determined to realise her priority of putting the children first in any new relationship:

---

4 Lone parents in Graham's (1987) study said they were better off as lone parents than they had been when married, commenting specifically, as did Mrs Bridges, on the substantial difference in the food bill when it has to include a family meal for a partner.

If anybody came into my household, no matter whether they're good or bad with money, I have to know that the children are being put first... I probably came out of the partnership with it as well, because although we had a lot more money... if they needed new shoes or something they would perhaps have to wait, where they wouldn't have to if he would have controlled his spending. He had to have a new car, he had to have a computer, he had to have all the things that other people had. (Mrs Bridges)

The egalitarian group was characterised by pooled allocation systems, joint or female control, and a view of breadwinning as a shared activity. A number of factors contributed to this: men's and women's labour market opportunities, women's experiences within a first marriage, and their experiences of providing for themselves and their children from an independent income.

The traditional group: reconstructing the male breadwinner

The couples in this group were characterised by a high degree of consensus between partners in valuing male breadwinner status highly. Women's views about their own labour market participation were influenced by an awareness of their partners views on the matter. The traditional divisions of labour between male wage-earner and female homemaker were reproduced in these couples' financial arrangements, which were predominantly whole wage systems (10 of the 14 couples) and subject to male control (11 of the 14 couples). Traditional divisions of labour to which they subscribed were mirrored by a conjugal contract which included female financial management and male financial privilege. Both roles carried responsibilities which were alluded to in these couples' descriptions of their financial arrangements. For instance, men described their wives approvingly as good managers, who would never do anything 'silly', thereby delineating a role which encompassed a mutual acceptance of personal restraint on her part in order to prioritise the children's needs. Women referred to their husbands as 'proud men' thereby signalling their identity as workers irrespective of their actual employment status. These couples' views on 'breadwinning' were influenced less by external circumstance than couples in other groups. Mr and Mrs Stirland's comments were typical:

> *It's a man's place to go out to work... I don't like women working... I wouldn't want my wife to go out to work to bring money in. She's the manager of the house. And she does a bloody good job.* (Mr Stirland)

> *He'd want to do something for his family* [ideally], *he'd be like the breadwinner, they call it. 'Breadwinner' – daft name that, isn't it? I mean it's still ours in the long run but Bill knows he's been a help to earn it. And he's been able to bring it in to the house... I brought up my children and Bill provides for us. Call me old-fashioned if you like.* (Mrs Stirland)

The women's deference to their partners' sensitivities on the subject was an expression of preserving the primacy of the single breadwinner model. Mr Short said: 'I think it's my job to provide for the family', and: 'I can't be relying on my wife – I'd end up asking for money'. His wife agreed with this – at least for the present. Although she experienced his control of the finances as necessary, it did have negative consequences for her:

> *I would like Chris to earn the money 'cos I know that he would like to be earning. To me, I don't mind being at home with Amanda... possibly when she's older I would like us both to be employed... I suppose because I would like us both to feel a little bit independent. Not to have to ask the other for money, either of us. Neither needing to ask the other one.* (Mrs Short)

For such couples, the fact that the man was unable to fulfil his role as breadwinner, at the time of the interview, was problematic for them, both in ideological as well as in financial terms. How did they cope with this? In part, some were aided by the fact that the family income was actually paid to the man. And, as we saw, it was men who cashed the Income Support/Jobseeker's Allowance, enabling them to follow the preferred allocation system of this group, the female whole wage, where the men 'hand over' their income to their partners. The fact that the money was paid to the man, that he cashed it and allocated it in this way was seen as wholly appropriate by each. This was not only because they felt that such a low income had to be managed by one person if it was to be managed effectively, but also because it validated the man's identity as the breadwinner.

In addition, various other strategies served to confirm and bolster the man's breadwinner identity. Mrs Parker and her partner had a two year old son and Mrs Parker was expecting their second child. She was keen to construct and maintain his identity not only as provider for herself and the baby, but as an effective and 'responsible' provider. She insisted that the Jobseeker's Allowance was his money, she made sure that he had any 'left-over' and she tried to give him authority by insisting that he did the 'phoning up' to negotiate terms of bill payment when they were short of money, although he was in fact noticeably less articulate than her. It appeared that enabling him to 'own' the money was her attempt to reward him for taking responsibility in the way she desired. This responsibility, in her eyes, was very much for herself *and* the baby. She wanted him to become a responsible parent as well as partner, and enabling him to spend on his daughter was one way of doing this. The concomitant part of this unwritten contract was that he should be able to have a night out with his mates. Benefits being paid to her would be contrary to her view of her partner as breadwinner:

> *It wouldn't be right coming all to me 'cos I'd be supporting him and he should be supporting me.* (Mrs Parker)

Mrs Hawley similarly gave her partner money to enable him to pay for things in public. Although she represented herself as very much in control of their finances, Mr Hawley gave an

excellent description of how male control operated through
the female whole wage:

> *Once the basic principles have been established, she knew
> basically what I would say anyway before she even discussed it
> with me...* [And the basic principles are what?]... *that I trust
> her with the money and she can basically do what she likes with
> it but she knows that she'll have to discuss it with me anyway
> out of like consideration or whatever. It's just an understanding
> really.* (Mr Hawley)

Mrs Hawley described how she saw it as appropriate that her
partner was financed to go out – and to pay his own way – for
a drink with his mates. She could never allow herself to
behave similarly:

> *I wouldn't do it 'cos it's their* [children's] *money and where's the
> money coming from?... I'll find it for him... his mates'll say
> 'Oh, come out', you know, 'We'll chip in.' And then I think: 'Oh
> no, he shouldn't do that'* [spend friends' money]. (Mrs Hawley)

As with Mr and Mrs Parker, this acted as a reward for being
the (putative) breadwinner. If he did not fulfil his part of this
contract, for example by failing effectively to 'bring in' the
money, he correspondingly suffered an attack on his identity,
as this account of a mix-up by the social security over his
benefit status illustrates:

> *Instead of getting £250, we got £53, and I thought: 'You're
> having a laugh'. And that was on a Saturday and I bought
> Tom's nappies and food, what I could, and I said to Laurence:
> 'Are you gonna go and sort this out?' And he said: 'Well I can't
> – they've told me that this is the way of things and that's all there
> is to it' And I really got stressed out and I went: 'You're bloody
> useless', I went mad, and I started crying. I said: 'The kids,
> what about the kids, what are they gonna have?'* (Mrs Hawley)

Mrs Hawley also explained why she, like Mrs Parker, was
reluctant to 'usurp' his authority as paterfamilias, despite
being perfectly capable of 'sorting it out' herself:

> *He went 'Well you go and get the money, you go and sort it out and you have the money put in your name, and you deal with it'. And I just felt I couldn't do that 'cos I'd be undermining him and that's showing him up... if you say 'Right, I'll have it all in my name', it makes the man look a bit* [hesitation] *useless. I think it's the tradition that the man's the head of the family, isn't he... so for me to go down there and throw a wobbler, it's undermining him... I see him for the person he is, not what I want him to be... but for his* [hesitation] – *how do you put it – masculinity – yeah? – he should be looked up to. The mainstay.* (Mrs Hawley)

Mr Hawley also saw it as appropriate that he should have authority invested in him:

> *At the moment 'cause I see the money given to me, counted out or whatever, I know exactly what's going on anyway before I give it to Judy... as things stand, I do have the responsibility of actually cashing it and what have you, er – doing certain things. If it was all down to Judy, I suppose I'd feel inadequate.* (Mr Hawley)

Interestingly, both women who protected their partner's authority in this way quietly kept some money separately, to which only they had access.

Men felt a sense of personal inadequacy about being unemployed. Two in particular highlighted the salience of male breadwinner identity, and these were where the traditional male breadwinner model had been 'spoiled' (Goffman, 1990) or reversed. In both these couples, one partner was the other's carer. Mrs and Mr Hoyle each had their 'own' benefit. Mr Hoyle was caring for his partner, and so received Invalid Care Allowance and Income Support. Mrs Hoyle received Disability Living Allowance and Child Benefit for their six children. She saw it as appropriate that he was still 'putting in' to the family, which preserved his 'bread-winner' identity in her eyes, whilst he referred to her specifically as the breadwinner because of her larger income:

*I treat it like she's the breadwinner so what she says goes...
Because she gets more money than I, you know, off all her books,
so I think she's the breadwinner.* (Mr Hoyle)

Mr Hoyle's ideal scenario was for the main income to come
from his wages, as this would have enabled him to provide for
his family:

*I think I would like to be, to come in from work and say: 'Here
y'are, love, here's your wages'.* (Mr Hoyle)

Mrs Hoyle retained much of 'the say' in financial matters
because the bulk of their income was officially paid to her. Mr
Hoyle, by having some income of 'his own' however, had
some say, and was protected from the risk he saw of his
partner 'throwing it back at him' that he wasn't earning. For
this reason, he wanted to retain some income in his own
right:

*If she was the main, you know, the main wage, wage person...
she's got another bullet for the gun... Like she would just say,
'Well I work for it, it's my money, I can do' – and what can you
say to that – nothing, could you really? – which is true if she is.*
(Mr Hoyle)

The fact that each contributed to the family income enabled
them both to have some say in how it was spent:

*Like now, it's our money 'cos I put in the kitty and Karen puts
in the kitty – it doesn't matter how much it is, it just goes in the
kitty. If I didn't have this Invalid Care Allowance it'd be all
Karen's money... it wouldn't feel so good for me because she'll
have the whole say. Like the way we think of it now – she puts
more than me in, but she says half and I say I put half in, so
we've got a half say each where it goes.* (Mr Hoyle)

Mrs Hoyle's least desired scenario was for the main income
to come from the woman's wages, not only because this was
seen as inappropriate for women, but also because it would
mean that the man was not making a proper contribution. It

was very important to Mrs Hoyle that they were both 'putting in' to the family financially:

> *Because it's not the woman's thing is it really? But like, we're both getting paid, so he's putting in as well. He's putting in for all the stuff and that. He's like, paying off the bills, and paying off the food... We're both doing it together. Because if a woman goes out to work, she's putting in all the money isn't she, because he's not really doing nothing – he's not really putting in for nothing is he really?* (Mrs Hoyle)

This couple provided the clearest indication *in practice* of a family's benefit income being paid individually, and illustrated the connection between being a *recipient* and having some control over allocation. The fact that his partner was the official recipient of the greater part of the income conferred on her the breadwinner identity in Mr Hoyle's eyes, but because he was the official recipient of some benefit income, he was entitled to some say in its allocation, thus curtailing her entitlement, as 'breadwinner', to all the say.

Another couple in this group derived their income from Disability Living Allowance and Invalid Care Allowance, but the wife was the carer. Mr Stanley wanted desperately to be his family's provider, but recognised that there was little likelihood of him being able to make financial provision through paid employment in the future. His wife said:

> *I think the man's always, for years and years, been the one that's supported the wife and family, the main supporter...* [And are you saying that you think that's how it should be, or you like that idea?] *No, it's the idea that's nice...* [For you or for him or for both?]*... For everyone... if we both had income coming in then obviously our money would be able to go further... my favourite would be both, combination, of the man and the woman's wages together... it'd be something that you actually went to work for and you earnt...* [Is it important to you ideally to have money in your own right?] *Yeah* [Can you say why it is?]*... Just to make me feel I've got a say on how my life is run a little bit... it would be nice if we could both return back to work*

and both have our own independence... it'd give myself
independence, my husband more dependence on himself. (Mrs
Stanley)

In this case, Mr Stanley's regular allocation of money for
tobacco or beer did not seem to be a way of rewarding a
'reconstructed' breadwinner identity, because both were only
too aware that this was unlikely ever to happen. This was a
cause of great psychological pain to them both. His 'pocket
money' appeared to act as a small compensation for his loss of
breadwinner identity, something he deserved because he
could not be the breadwinner.

For all in this group, however, the model of male breadwinner continued to operate as the defining force behind the
allocation of household income.

The male-dominated group: ambivalent breadwinning

This group was distinguishable from the others by a degree of
ambivalence towards breadwinning. This manifested itself in a
number of factors in the interaction between the partners in
these couples. Four of the five couples had only one child
aged 22 months. (One had a child of three as well as the 22-
month-old, and one woman was currently expecting a second
child.) Regardless of how long the couples had been together,
they had only relatively recently become parents. For four of
the women this appeared to be at a particularly vulnerable
stage in their lives.

The two men in receipt of Jobseeker's Allowance had been
unemployed since the birth of the child, and they overtly
rejected male breadwinner status. Nevertheless, for them, as
for all the men in this group, spending on the kinds of thing
they valued personally appeared to have been maintained
rather than adjusted in response to the additional financial
demands of parenthood. These additional pressures on the
household income were also taking place in the context of a
drop in income, which was quite substantial for three couples,
as the women, prior to childbirth, had been able to earn as
much as, or more than, their husbands.

There was also a dissonance between men's views of their own breadwinner identity and the women's perceptions of who should be the breadwinner. Men's espousing of breadwinner identity was ambivalent, while the women had clear expectations of their husbands as sole breadwinners. Women had very little enthusiasm to share breadwinning. The one woman who was employed had gone back to work very reluctantly, when their child was six months old, and her husband had been disqualified from benefit. The Family Credit they now received was based on her earnings. Two women undervalued their own status as wage-earners despite contrary evidence from their own employment histories, and two were positive about wanting to remain homemakers in the future.

Most of these couples used a pooled management system, but the men were exclusively in control of the finances. Contradictory accounts signalled a struggle around which definition of breadwinner identity was holding sway at the time. The deference paid by women to partners in whom they vested authority was predicated on their expectations of him as breadwinner, but this was sometimes met by men's own ambivalence towards their ability or inclination to assume that identity. The contestation was enacted as women tried, and failed, to control their partners' individual spending, and as men subverted their partners' attempts to manage the income effectively, by using credit. Tension arose from the individual spending in which men engaged as real or putative breadwinners, regardless of their own ambivalence towards the provider role they had been ascribed.

Mr Holland, whose high levels of personal spending on hobbies had led to heavy debts, fiercely rejected traditional notions of the male breadwinner. His espousal of the rights, but not the responsibilities, that go with male breadwinning, meant that his wife had become the reluctant breadwinner. He said:

I don't like this idea of the breadwinner of the family... I have always hated this Ealing comedyish sort of – the wife at home

> *with a housecoat on and slaving over a stove all day, and the*
> *chap coming home from the pit or whatever – I don't think that's*
> *relevant to the 20th century... certainly in the 90s I think we*
> *should be looking at a family as a unit rather than the man's*
> *wages or the woman's wages or anything – equal status rule.*
> (Mr Holland)

This 'equal status rule' appeared to apply rather differently to him and his wife, however, so that she had the right to earn the money but not to spend it, while he had the right to spend it without earning it.

For two of the couples, the relative ages of the partners appeared to be a significant factor in the women's inability to control their husband's spending. Mrs Thackeray and Mrs Norton had married men ten years older than themselves. Both men had been in partnerships before, and, as we saw in Chapter 3, both men had incurred large 'individual' debts.

The idea that Mr Thackeray's wife might be able to earn more than him appeared to threaten his own breadwinner identity. He did not see why he should go out to work himself if his wife could demonstrate the ability to earn equally. However, as a route to more disposable income for him, the idea of her undertaking paid work outside the home did have a certain appeal:

> *That's interesting actually. If she was working as well then*
> *there's a chance that – I think she would still deal with all the*
> *main things like all the bills – but that would probably just allow*
> *me to have a little bit more free money to pursue my own*
> *personal endeavours... although obviously she's young and that,*
> *I know she wouldn't stray or anything, and she knows the*
> *situation if she did... I don't think I would actually mind her*
> *working... I mean, I don't see why I should have to go out to*
> *work every day if my wife could do just the same job for the same*
> *money and get double the income at the end of the month... if my*
> *wife was happy to work then I would be totally consenting.*
> *Providing it wasn't in something like a brothel.* (Mr Thackeray)

Mrs Norton's need to see her husband as the provider upon whom she could depend was very strong indeed. He held traditional gender role views which made him the ideal partner for this young woman who had come to London, got 'chucked out' of her job, met, fell in love with and married her husband, all within the space of a week, and who had only ever wanted to be 'a happy little woman':

> *I feel responsible, I don't want him to have to sit there worrying about being a non, a dysfunctioning breadwinner, whereas it's not fair that he should find it his fault. On the other hand, I've been criticised by my family for becoming pregnant, not once, but twice... all I ever wanted really was little people of my own, to be happy... it's lovely having a little person of my own and having Robert [husband] – I don't like being alone, so it's nice... I like him to be able to have things because he's been so good to me – whenever possible it would be so nice for me to be able to let him have what he likes. And in a way trying to please, 'cos I would like to keep my husband happy – I like to be a little woman – I'm just happy if all my family is happy – if I can put little burnt offerings on the table and whiz round with the Hoover with my hair tied up in a dandy knot and be a happy little woman.* (Mrs Norton)

Mr Norton recognised that his wife wanted and needed him to be the provider and that her handing him the financial responsibility was symbolic of this:

> *She was more happier having the financial side of our relationship taken away from her. Well, she gave it away because she was happier that way. She hasn't gone into great detail about her financial past but she had, apparently, bad experiences with her ex-boyfriends.* (Mr Norton)

His acceptance of this responsibility was a more tenuous affair. He found it a great pressure, but could not allow himself any recriminations:

> *It's a large pressure because our financial situation isn't getting better. It gets worse, and because we're on limited means we can only do 'x' amount of things with 'x' amount of money. I keep things inside and I tend to bottle things up very much, which is probably why I've got an ulcer* [pause] *and it is, it is, it's, it is a great pressure... I say to her, I never had an ulcer before I met her* [laughter]*... I would never, ever blame her for it.* (Mr Norton)

He was to some extent trapped by his sense of what he 'ought' to do in a role he would really much rather not have had:

> *Well I see the fact that I should – I don't know whether it's an old-fashioned view – the fact that it's me, as far as I'm concerned, that has the responsibility of doing that, of being the provider and making sure that we get through.* (Mr Norton)

Undertaking this responsibility on a very low income involved such pressure that the commitment to this 'old-fashioned view' became more flexible, and the idea of working at home on DIY projects became much more attractive than any preference for breadwinner status he had felt obliged to express:

> *I don't know whether it's supposed to be a new man... I would be quite happy if Amy could go out and find a job that would keep both of us and the children, it wouldn't bother me in the slightest, it would not be a threat to my manhood* [laughing] *for her to do that. I see myself as a househusband, I really do. I love looking after children. I'm, literally, a home-maker.* (Mr Norton)

In these 'new' young families, women's 'dependency' and the need to be 'supported' by their husbands was at a high point. Men clearly felt the pressures of this responsibility, and were ambivalent in practice about meeting its requirements.

SUMMARY

- Male control was derived from different models of bread-winner identity: for the egalitarian group, it was constituted by joint activity, the traditional group attempted to reconstruct male breadwinner identity, and the male-dominated group was marked by ambivalence about breadwinner identity.
- Male control was a crucial determinant of financial distribution patterns, with a repeat pattern of male-incurred debt, via the use of credit facilities, being a noticeable feature.
- Couples in the egalitarian group were mostly in receipt of Family Credit, and used pooling systems. Couples in the traditional group were predominantly on Income Support/Jobseeker's Allowance, and used the female whole wage and housekeeping allowance. Those in the male-dominated group were predominantly on Family Credit and used a mixture of male and female managed pools, and independent management.
- In some cases, payment of Income Support/Jobseeker's Allowance to men reinforced the construction of a male breadwinner identity which was associated with greater female disadvantage. In other cases, the payment of Family Credit to women was associated with an egalitarian distribution of resources. For two women, receipt of FC was associated with independent forms of management and a less egalitarian distribution of resources.
- Elements of segregation and independent management highlighted the dangers of treating the systems as discrete categories, and revealed the importance of the source and the recipient of income in a way not encompassed by the typology.
- One component of an egalitarian distribution of financial resources was the degree of control exerted by women as a result of experiences in a first marriage and subsequent experience of an income in their own right as lone parents.

- One component of an inegalitarian distribution of financial resources was the stage in partners' marital careers, with new young mothers being particularly susceptible to their partners' inclinations to access disproportionate amounts of household income as personal spending.
- Breadwinning ideology was a powerful determinant of the intra-household distribution of income, but the interaction between labour market constraints, payment of benefits, and partners' life-experiences was also significant. In some instances, this meant that, contrary to suggestions in earlier research, it was the women's attitudes which were the more salient in determining breadwinning models and allocation patterns.

Chapter 7

Methods of payment of social security benefits

In the light of policy debates on alternative methods of paying social security, and in order to make clear the connections between the ways in which money enters the household (that is, its source as social security income paid to a particular recipient) and its allocation and distribution, we investigated interviewees' responses to alternative ways families might receive their income. This chapter presents men's and women's responses to a number of different income scenarios, and their views on alternative models of benefit payment.

Interviewees were presented with 'vignettes' of different income scenarios which referred in turn to income derived from wages and income derived from benefit, and they were asked to consider and comment upon these. For each of these two sources, they were presented with scenarios of a family's main income being paid wholly to the man, wholly to the woman, or derived from a combination of both as recipients. As we saw, interviewees' responses to scenarios of men's and women's earned income formed the basis of the analysis on breadwinning presented in Chapter 6. Responses to the scenarios in which benefit income is paid to different recipients are presented here.

In addition, couples were asked for their views on the implications of splitting Income Support/Jobseeker's

Allowance, or on the payment of Family Credit through the pay packet. A few couples had experiences of receiving both kinds of benefit, and they were asked for their views on both ways of payment.

THE SIGNIFICANCE OF BEING THE BENEFIT RECIPIENT

Interviewees were asked to respond to and express a preference for scenarios in which an imaginary family, wholly reliant on benefit, has that benefit paid to the man, to the woman, or to a combination of both. Responses fell into three categories: no preference; a preference for payment to the man; a preference for payment to the woman. Results are shown by 'group' and by current benefit type.

Table 7.1   Preferred recipient for benefit payment:
            no preference

	Egalitarian	Traditional	Male-dominated	Total
M	6	8	2	16
F	5	4	1	10
Total	11	12	3	26

	IS/JSA	FC	Total
M	6	10	16
F	2	8	10
Total	8	18	26

Twenty-six people said they had no preference as to who received the benefit (Table 7.1), because it was felt that it would make no difference to the money's allocation. There were 16 men who chose this option: 10 were in receipt of Family Credit currently and they were spread across the three groups; 10 women had no preference: eight of these were in receipt of Family Credit, and they too were spread across the three groups, although there was only one in the male-dominated group.

Table 7.2   **Preferred recipient for benefit payment: the man**

	Egalitarian	Traditional	Male-dominated	Total
M	4	3	3	10
F	2	8	1	11
Total	6	11	4	21

	IS/JSA	FC	Total
M	5	5	10
F	8	3	11
Total	13	8	21

The method of Income Support/Jobseeker's Allowance payment preferred by 21 people was for it to go wholly to the man (Table 7.2). There were 10 men and 11 women who chose this, and this response came mostly from current Income Support/Jobseeker's Allowance recipients. Of the Family Credit recipients, there were five men and three women who chose this. Again, those opting for this were spread across the three groups, but women tended to cluster in the traditional group, and only two women in the egalitarian group chose the man as the recipient as the preferred option.

Table 7.3   **Preferred recipient for benefit payment: the woman**

	Egalitarian	Traditional	Male-dominated	Total
M	1	2	0	3
F	5	2	3	10
Total	6	4	3	13

	IS/JSA	FC	Total
M	1	2	3
F	2	8	10
Total	3	10	13

The option favoured by fewest people (13) was for the benefit to be paid solely to the woman (Table 7.3), but the patterns here were striking. They were mostly Family Credit recipients, and mostly women. As far as the representation across the three groups was concerned, none of the five men in the male-dominated group chose this option, but three of the five women did. Comments by these women were revealing. Mrs Thackeray had represented herself as having financial control, but could not curb her husband's personal credit spending. The fact that her control was more nominal than real was confirmed by her choosing in this exercise to have Jobseeker's Allowance benefit paid to her. She saw the other two options as reducing her control:

> *I don't think I'd have the same control rights over it... if it was paid through giro it might change things, because he would have access to the money and he might not be very keen on giving it to me. With* [a combination] *I think that would be a problem, because he would definitely have half of it, and it would be, just, getting the money back to cover the necessary household things.* (Mrs Thackeray)

Where control was joint, as in the egalitarian group, responses suggested that men and women saw the actual recipient of benefit as insignificant for its distribution. Where couples were currently wholly reliant on Income Support/Jobseeker's Allowance they were likely to choose the option which reflected their current experience of benefit being paid to the man. Where control was male and resulted in female disadvantage, women were likely to express a preference for benefit being paid to themselves, but none of the men in these couples expressed this preference.

These findings suggest that in households where there are factors which pre-dispose couples towards an inegalitarian distribution of income, the recipient of that income is particularly significant. As the following section demonstrates, couples' responses to the idea of splitting a family's income, so that half is paid to the man and half to the woman, confirmed that the connection between being the recipient of benefit income and having control over its disposal is seen as crucial in such households.

SPLIT PAYMENT OF INCOME SUPPORT/JOBSEEKER'S ALLOWANCE

As some couples had received Income Support/Jobseeker's Allowance in the past, they were also asked to consider the idea of split payments of Income Support/Jobseeker's Allowance. Responses were drawn from 23 women and 16 men. The model of a family's benefit being paid half to the man and half to the woman received little support from the couples, although it was recognised that creating policy as a way of engineering the distribution of money within the household is a complex business:

> *That's a hard one... unless either one of the partners who looks after the children are getting hard-done-by – go down to Social and say: 'Look, this is my situation and you're gonna have to give me the bulk of the money and him some.' And then again, it's up to that person, if they're strong – 'cos they're rocking the boat, aren't they, in their own home, and the other partner could get quite nasty – it's hard really.* (Mrs Hawley)

> *It's a real hornets' nest, that one, isn't it?* (Mrs Barber)

Often respondents said that it would merely create unwelcome administrative and financial management complications for themselves, but were much more strongly opposed to the idea for other people they knew. All of those who felt it would be a bad idea, either for themselves or for others, were classified as a negative response.

In total, 16 women and 13 men thought it a bad suggestion; four women and three men were neutral about it, seeing it as 'pointless' or as making no difference to them; and three women thought it would be a good idea. A stronger reason than administrative inconvenience for not favouring the idea was that it would validate personal 'ownership' of an income designed for the family, in some cases with possibly damaging implications for the benefit available to the women.

Some interviewees recognised in the proposal an attempt to protect women and children from being disadvantaged, but felt that it would at best lead to arguments, and at worst encourage men to regard their half of the household income as belonging to them individually, leaving women to provide for themselves and the children on half an income – what Mrs Short described as 'a colossal minus for her either way'. There was a recognition, however, that for women who suffered severe financial deprivation within their current allocation systems, receiving half the household income would represent an improvement:

> *It would help for the women whose husbands didn't come home with their benefits. I do know a lot of people actually that get it in their name, and keep them very, very short. But not themselves short. So in that case I'd rather it be split for them reasons. This is not for mine and Paul's, personally, but for every man and woman in the country.* (Mrs Stanley)

For many, the suggestion of splitting the Income Support/ Jobseeker's Allowance in half represented a threat to the shared ideology of marriage, and challenged the idea that the money actually belonged to neither partner. It was given to them *because of the family,* to support the family. It was seen as vital therefore to preserve the idea that the money was not individually but collectively owned. Paying half the household income to each partner was seen as validating the idea of 'own' money and as allowing the man to spend all of 'his' money independently.

Among the minority who supported this split payment were eight respondents in the egalitarian group, currently in receipt of Family Credit, who had claimed Income Support in the past. Three of these were women who had been lone parents after the break-up of a previous relationship. One woman recounted having to ask her partner for money for personal hygiene products. Her current partnership afforded her access to *part* of the Jobseeker's Allowance in addition to her Child Benefit, and this improvement on her earlier situation led her to express only mild support for the individualisation of benefits. She reflected on the fact that such a change would mean having some money of her own, and she felt this 'would be nice'.

The other two women who supported the idea were the households receiving Disability Living Allowance and Invalid Care Allowance as well as Income Support, which represented an approximation of the scenario they were being asked to consider – a family's income derived from benefit, some of which is paid to the man and some of which is paid to the woman. This appeared to sharpen the perceived importance of entitlement in one's own right, validated by being the actual recipient of the income, in the same way as is the case with earned income:

> *It would feel different [if the woman received benefit in her own right]... she'd feel like she's still getting something rather than taking it off him or having to ask... it would give 'em their self esteem back wouldn't it?... rather than me having to say, can you sign that so I can go up the Post Office to get some of my money, something that I'm entitled to as well... in the past I've said, why are you printing down my name when I'm your agent – it hasn't got it printed down, so I've got to let you sign for me to go and get my benefits for myself and my children.* (Mrs Stanley)

In discussing how they would be affected if changes *were* actually made so that benefit was paid wholly to the woman, or split between the man and the woman, some modified their responses in favour of payment to women. In other words, when respondents inferred that such a change might be seriously under consideration, payment of all or most of the benefit to women in families where there are children was seen as having a logical and acceptable rationale, that the woman is the one responsible for the children's welfare:

Well, it all depends why they're doing it... they could be doing it to stop the fella splashing it up against a brick wall. Well that wouldn't be wrong, giving them half each, would it?... If there was kids involved, the woman should get the majority of the money then. (Mr Rickards)

I think the woman should get more because she looks after the kids more. (Mr Hoyle)

I suppose it would depend on if they had children, because obviously the woman usually sorts out kids' needs so she probably needs a bit more than what the father or the partner would. (Mr Stirland)

I do know relationships where the man's got the bulk of the money and before they've come home they've gone in the pub and had a good old skinful, so if you've got a relationship like that, then the woman should have her own money in her own right... three-quarters of it, 'cos it's the woman that sorts out the children as well – a man won't. (Mrs Hawley)

It also became clear that the job-seeking requirement attached to the receipt of benefit had influenced respondents' views towards payment to the man:

I'm not the type of lad who thinks a man's better than a woman or should be treated better than a woman... if they're gonna pay her because they have to pay her, well fair enough, they pay her. It just so happens that the Government's put me in the category, saying the man is the main one who goes down and signs on, so so be it. (Mr Barlow)

If it was paid wholly to me, I'd then feel responsible to go and get a job because I'm getting the benefit. It's a Jobseeker's Allowance, therefore I should be going to find a job. (Mrs Norton)

For women themselves, the experience of being, or having been, the recipient of Income Support/Jobseeker's Allowance in their own right also validated the principle of having one's own money. Nevertheless, the fears of both men and women, that to individualise payment of a family's benefit would risk leaving women with insufficient money to meet their family's needs, outweighed the more positive aspects which they identified.

PAYING FAMILY CREDIT THROUGH THE PAY PACKET

Family Credit couples (plus two Income Support/Jobseeker's Allowance couples) were asked what they thought about the idea of paying Family Credit through the pay packet, rather than directly to the recipient. This proposal received little support from either men or women. Men were more likely to be neutral about the idea, and women more likely to express outright opposition. Men also tended to reject the idea because they felt that the part it currently played in their household allocation system was effective:

> *I don't think there's anything wrong with the way it is, to be honest, so if it ain't broke don't try to fix it... it's easy at the moment 'cos she can just walk up to the Post Office and she's got the cash there.* (Mr Gibson)

> *That would spoil our little routine, but in principle we wouldn't have any worries with it... I think I would really prefer it to stay as it is now.* [Can you tell me why?] *Well if it was to get muddled in with me wages which it would do... well we're a stickler with this now, it's worked for us for so long.* (Mr Rickards)

Other men unequivocally rejected the idea either because they did not trust employers, or because they were aware that in the hands of men less fair than they saw themselves, it would not be properly allocated to the family as intended:

> *I wouldn't like that. Because I wouldn't trust my employer. They're not very good on being totally honest with your wages. They keep knocking bits off, hoping that you won't notice and even if it be 50p or whatever... it's still money gone. I would feel better if it stayed the way it is. I would prefer it if Louise could*

> *get it because it really is needed and it would probably end up getting lost in or eaten up by other things.* (Mr Macmillan)

> *I don't like it because my employer would somehow swindle a way of getting some of that for themselves. I like to think that it would be paid separately by book or by direct debit to either my account or my wife's account, whichever, I don't mind now.* (Mr Thackeray)

> *I feel it should be kept at the Post Office, so that the wife, who is at home, can go and collect it and buy the necessary stuff just to live for that week... I do feel that the wife should be able to go and collect that cash.* (Mr Clark)

> *One bloke might say, 'You're not having a penny, here's twenty quid, I'm going down the pub tonight'... And that's robbing the family isn't it?... if you've got a really nasty piece of work who beats his wife up and goes out drinking every night solidly, and all of a sudden he's got that straight in his account!* (Mr Morris)

Women across all three groups were much more strongly against the idea than men, although Mr Williams, a man in a 'role swap' couple, who used the Family Credit as a housekeeping allowance, was also vehemently opposed. Women valued the current payment methods because the money came *directly to them,* it was *guaranteed weekly* and *separate from their husband's wages.* Their weekly cash payment was a vital budgeting tool:

> *The idea's rubbish!... from our point of view knowing that we get that money each week makes it easier to handle rather than getting a lump sum each month, at least we know there's something there each week rather than having to wait a month... I would prefer to have it weekly.* (Mrs Williams)

> *No I'm not keen because we've got into a routine now where we've got everything worked out to our advantage... we've got a guaranteed, really a guaranteed amount of money every week.* (Mr Williams)

No I don't like that idea. I like going to the post office and knowing it's there… when I get the Family Credit you see it goes on the bills…I wouldn't like it coming with his pay. I like to get it separate. (Mrs Rickards)

You've got that little bit there like a security-type thing… keep that separate so that if you need it, it's there. I just like lump sums… If it come in his wages it would be in dribs and drabs and it wouldn't really make a lot of difference… it'd just class as his wages. (Ms Morris)

No! [laughing] *because if it was paid through the employee's pay packet then it would just get swallowed up… if I'm short, if I've spent all of Tony's wages then I can buy food with it.* (Mrs Macmillan)

They could say right we're gonna pay it through wages and then not pay it. You know, there's no guarantee that you're gonna get it in with your wages. So the book, it's like, it's just guaranteed money. (Mrs Scorton)

Women were also aware that if paid via the wage packet, men could keep it for themselves rather than allocating it to the family:

No way! No… it's knowing that I'm going to get that money on a Tuesday and it will cover the nappies, the electric. I can go out and pay those bills on the Tuesday knowing that I've got the cash in my purse and not having to go through the bank account to get it. I wouldn't want it through his wages. (Mrs Clark)

If you're getting Family Credit and it's the man that's working I suppose some men would think, I'm earning it, it's my money. When you get Family Credit now, it goes to the woman even if it's the man that's working, so at least the woman knows she's got something there each week rather than having to ask her husband for it you know. (Mrs Williams)

Some women in the least egalitarian households, in which the Family Credit was paid into a jointly accessed account, saw it as changing little. In contrast, for Mrs Ripley, whose Family

Credit constituted the only money to which she had access, the idea was very unwelcome. She was perfectly happy with their current arrangements, but this was because the Family Credit represented independence to her, and she hated the idea of having to ask her husband for money, which this change would entail. For Mrs Dakin, too, the Family Credit represented the only money over which she had control:

> *No, I like getting it because it's something that's my responsibility that I do and something that I go and get. I do like it the way it is now and I do like it weekly rather than monthly or anything like that...* [And is the fact that you would prefer it to stay the way it is, coming to you, to do with the fact that it comes to you, or to do with the fact that it's weekly and it offers you something every week rather than every month?] *I think it's a bit of both actually 'cos it's something that's mine – I do feel that the Family Credit is for me, and Jay's wages are his, and Rose's Child Benefit's hers. I just feel it's something that's for me. Although it doesn't go on me, it goes on other things, it's something that's mine.* (Mrs Dakin)

Her husband felt that women should be able to retain 'that little comfort zone':

> *No I don't agree with that... to have it paid into an account where at the moment my wages are the only thing that goes in there, and to see those lumped in on my wages as well, I think is quite demeaning... mums used to work and now they've changed career and they just work at home and look after the child. They still have to have a mind and they have to be able to think about things, so having that little comfort zone of being able to manage that little pot of money that they have – it sounds terribly patronising, but to manage that little bit of money that they have to put towards their child – I think to take that away from them would be wrong.* (Mr Dakin)

The most heartfelt plea for the continuation of Family Credit as a benefit paid to women came from Mrs Smales, a member of the egalitarian group, who before her current partnership had had experience of a male-controlled female whole wage system and then of lone parenthood.

> *I think any benefit that a woman is relying on should be paid directly to the woman, and should not go to the man at all... I don't think it should happen like that – absolutely not, definitely... I'm only thinking about the wives that wouldn't be able to rely on their husbands. I really think it is a bad idea for benefits – such an important thing, that is – after all, these things are paid to people with children. And that money is for the children, and women just think about their children more than men do. I really think that women should be paid any benefits that those children are entitled to, and not the men.* (Mrs Smales)

SUMMARY

- There was only minimal support from women for benefits to be paid individually to them. Support came from those women who had had experience of independent benefit income, and women in the least egalitarian group.
- Both men and women identified a need in some families reliant on benefit to protect the interests of children against men's personal spending, and saw payment to women as serving this end. Where interviewees surmised that changes in favour of paying Income Support/Jobseeker's Allowance to women were on the policy agenda, they invoked a logic in support of such a proposal, which cited women's major responsibility for the care of children.
- Individualised payment of Income Support/Jobseeker's Allowance, however, was seen as threatening a definition of this income as collectively owned money paid specifically to support the family. In that it was seen as potentially validating the idea of individual ownership, there was a perceived risk that the man would spend all of 'his' money individually.

- The proposal to pay Family Credit through the pay packet received little support, and considerable opposition. Men's opposition related to their mistrust of employers as well as an acknowledgement of the positive aspects of women's receipt of family credit within their current patterns of financial management. They also cited the risk of Family Credit being swallowed up by male-incurred debt. Women's opposition centred upon the perceived advantages of current methods of payment, which gave them income which was *guaranteed,* paid *directly to them,* came weekly, was *accessed via the Post Office* and was *separate from their partner's wages.* Women in inegalitarian households for whom Family Credit was the only income to which they had access, were particularly opposed to the idea.

Chapter 8

Conclusions and policy implications

METHODS OF PAYING SOCIAL SECURITY BENEFITS

Social security policy has traditionally treated the household unit for which means tested benefits are paid as a single entity, without problematising financial relations between the individuals who comprise that unit. Nevertheless, the issue of to whom benefit should be paid has erupted on the political stage on a number of occasions in relation to benefits for children, namely Family Allowances/Child Benefit and, more recently, Family Credit. Earlier studies supported by the Joseph Rowntree Foundation, and also the Equal Opportunities Commission (Esam and Berthoud, 1991; Roll, 1991; Smith, 1991; Lister, 1992; Duncan *et al*, 1994), also served to underline the saliency of the issue of the intra-household distribution of income for social security policy, with particular reference to the choice of benefit unit for the assessment and payment of benefits. More generally, economists and social policy analysts have made the case for a conceptualisation of poverty in terms of individual rights to a minimum level of resources, questioning the acceptability of the dependency of one partner, typically the woman, on the other.

At European level, the European Commission (1997) has promoted the case for the 'individualisation' of social security benefits on a number of occasions, most recently in a 1997 Communication in which it argued that 'individualisation is in line with the general trend towards a greater autonomy of the individual'. In domestic politics, the issue of the intra-household distribution is highly relevant to current reviews of the tax-benefit system and could be said to represent a point of convergence between the briefs of the current Secretary of State for Social Security and Minister for Women.

The present study provided some evidence of what social security recipients themselves think about these issues. It also confirmed some of the findings of previous research on low income families and on patterns of household financial allocation, as well as throwing new light on gendered patterns of income control, management and allocation within families receiving social security.

It demonstrated the enduring nature of a distribution pattern in which women are more likely to shoulder the burden of managing a low income single-handedly, while at the same time experiencing higher levels of financial deprivation and less access to personal spending money than men, in order to prioritise their children's needs. It revealed, in a way not encompassed by previous research, that both the source and the recipient of income were highly significant for its allocation. The methods of paying social security income influenced its distribution.

COUPLES' PERCEPTIONS OF THEIR INCOME AND EXPENDITURE

Male wages were seen by both partners as constituting bread-winning, and as conferring on the man entitlement to individual spending. Some men took advantage of this and some did not. Where the man was unemployed, some couples jointly reconstructed his identity as the breadwinner and reinstated his entitlement to personal spending money. Others wholly reliant on benefit income saw it as collectively owned, and a few did not feel that it was rightfully theirs at all. For some, women's wages, and benefits paid directly to women, also constituted breadwinning, and thereby conferred decision-making powers on women. The examination of men's and women's perceptions of different sources of income, and the meanings they attached to them, underlined how social security policy can touch upon sensitive areas of personal and family identity.

Couples' conceptualisations of the distinction between individual and collective expenditure were related to gender roles. Consumption too was gendered. These conceptualisations legitimated men's personal spending and defined women's collective expenditure, for example on children, as personal. In addition, the burden of empty time for some unemployed men led them to spend on activities such as DIY and car maintenance, which had a dual definition of individual and collective expenditure.

GENDER AND THE MANAGEMENT AND CONTROL OF HOUSEHOLD INCOME

The women in this study reported higher levels of 'going without' than men, and there was convincing evidence of higher levels of personal spending by men than by women. While confirming patterns of credit and debt documented by earlier studies, this study also showed how the use of credit was gendered, acting as a significant route to men's personal spending. In practice, therefore, the distinction between individual and collective expenditure did not accord in a straightforward way with that drawn in the existing literature. However, the paradigm remained a useful one in understanding the differential distribution of resources.

Women's prioritising of children meant that they rarely engaged in individual spending, even from sources of income seen as theirs to allocate. At the same time, women carried the major burden of the worry and stress associated with managing a low income, particularly acute where it involved debt-management. Men's worries, which had not formed the focus of past studies, typically centred upon their ability to secure employment with high enough wages adequately to support their families. Many men explicitly acknowledged that they had been relieved of the burden of managing a low income because their partners undertook the task. However, it was also a source of stress for those few men who did undertake it themselves.

EXPLAINING DISTRIBUTION PATTERNS

As in earlier research, male control of the household income was associated with female disadvantage, although not exclusively. The couples' age and the stage in their life cycle also emerged as particularly salient factors impacting on the intra-household distribution of income.[5] In particular, some of the mechanisms and strategies through which male control operated, or was circumscribed, within female-managed systems, rested on particular features of the couples' relationship, their relative ages, and the desire of individuals for degrees of dependence or independence, sometimes reflecting earlier experiences.

Breadwinner identity remained a powerful predictor of the distribution of household income, but in a context of new forms of paid work and family life. This group of families, however, did not subscribe to a single model of breadwinning. The distribution of household income was therefore determined by the relationship between different models of breadwinning subscribed to by couples,[6] and by the stage couples had reached in their marital career.

Especially significant factors were: couples' perceptions of what constituted breadwinning in their current circumstances and how far female labour market participation might contribute to this; women who were relatively new mothers and married to older men; and women's prior experience of

---

5   Pahl (1989) and Vogler and Pahl (1993) touched only tangentially on 'life-stage' influences, by reference to 'early socialisation', using data on allocation systems used by respondents' parents, and by tracing generational shifts.

6   With the payment of social security benefits functioning significantly in the way these models were constituted.

lone parenthood and an income in their own right, which had led to a valuing of a degree of independence and control within marriage.

Gender role ideology, particularly in relation to men's and women's paid work, has featured significantly in previous research in this area, as it does in our own research, but here, the influence of women's experiences, attitudes and activity influenced couples' decisions rather more than suggested in previous studies. Couples' capacity for change in the light of their life-experiences suggested an 'interactive' relationship between attitudes, economic circumstances and behaviour.

The life experiences partners brought to their relationship, particularly women's experience of lone parenthood and an independent income, played an important role in this interaction, and highlighted women's agency within the family and the employment market. This should caution against an over-emphasis on male attitudes, or on a particular, unassailable model of breadwinning, as explanations for patterns of financial allocation, and confirms the need to be sensitive to indicators and sources of change, however slow the pace may be.

Our study therefore confirmed the importance of two-way interactions between men and women in a partnership, and between couples and the labour market. It also revealed the ways in which methods of paying social security benefits shaped couples' responses to the different elements of these interactions, by coinciding with, reinforcing, or constraining the decisions couples made as part of their adaptations.

POLICY IMPLICATIONS

The present study sheds light, therefore, on a number of topical policy issues, although not always in a totally unambiguous way. Where it is perhaps clearest is in the evidence it provides for the importance of benefits for children being paid to the caring parent, still mainly the mother. It confirms earlier research, both historical and contemporary, underlining how women's responsibility for meeting children's needs means that benefits for children are more likely to be spent on children, if channelled direct to the mother.

The study also demonstrates the potential importance of a *minimum wage* for families supported by one or more low paid wage-earners. Wages were patently valued over means-tested benefits as a source of household income. A degree of anger against employers paying low wages, as well as distrust of them, was translated into spontaneous support for the idea of a minimum wage among a number of both men and women in receipt of Family Credit.

Despite the resentment that wages needed topping up, the importance attached by mothers in particular to *Family Credit* as a weekly budgeting tool in providing for the family must cast serious doubt on any proposal to replace it with some form of *Earned Income Tax Credit or Working Families Tax Credit* (a proposal that had not yet been mooted when the study was undertaken). Following the American model, this would be received by the wage-earner.[7] In about three-quarters of couples receiving Family Credit, this would mean a transfer of resources from the woman to the man.

Couples' responses to the idea of paying Family Credit through the paypacket, as originally intended by the Conservative Government, indicated that such a move would be unpopular among both men and women. They saw this as removing a vital source of direct weekly income for mothers, available in cash from the Post Office, that enabled them to budget to meet their families' needs with a degree of security. Moreover, our study suggests that it can play an important role in contributing to a more egalitarian distribution of income in families reliant on a low wage.

The announcement by the Chancellor of the Exchequer (12 February 1998) that couples would be able to choose whether the credit was paid through the pay packet or as a

---

7   For a critical discussion of the earned income tax credit, see Meadows (1997), Walker and Wiseman (1997) and Mendelson (1998).

cash benefit goes some way to meeting the concerns about the impact of a Working Family Tax Credit on the distribution of income within families. However, the evidence of this study regarding the dynamics of financial decision-making raises serious questions as to how 'real' this choice would be in safeguarding the credit as money to be spent on the children. In the most inegalitarian families, women are unlikely to have the power to exercise the choice in their own favour. Even in other families, there may be a reluctance to challenge the presumption that this is money to top up the man's low wages. Therefore, it is essential that the choice is presented in such a way as to legitimate the existing notion that the money is for the family and for the mother to control.

Our findings likewise endorse those of earlier studies demonstrating the importance of *Child Benefit* as a source of income paid to mothers to meet the needs of children, especially where, as in most cases in our study, this is paid through a weekly order book. One possible policy implication therefore is that a significant increase in Child Benefit should be seen as an important part of the government's minimum wage strategy. It would counteract what could otherwise be an unfortunate gendered side-effect of a minimum wage: that in one-earner couples the wage-earner's pay rise would be translated into a cut in the carer's Family Credit.[8] Moreover, in the context of the introduction of an Earned Income Tax Credit, a significant increase in Child Benefit would be vital in protecting some of the money currently paid directly to mothers to meet family needs.

Couples' positive attitudes towards Child Benefit, and to a lesser extent Family Credit, contrasted with more negative

---

8 As highlighted earlier, in the majority of two-parent families in receipt of Family Credit, the main wage-earner is the man, and it is in this context that measures would be needed to ensure that a minimum wage did not adversely affect women's ability to care for their families. In the broader context, as the majority of low paid workers are women, a minimum wage would benefit women, although the level at which it is set is obviously crucial (see Millar, Webb and Kemp, 1997).

perceptions of *Income Support/income-related Jobseeker's Allowance*. What was striking was the extent to which recipients expressed a sense of being stigmatised by receiving the latter benefits and of the money not really belonging to them. Such feelings are likely to be exacerbated if politicians and the media refer in pejorative terms to benefit claimants as inhabiting a 'dependency culture'.

Couples' sense of not really being entitled to the money may be one factor which helps explain why so few women favoured individual ownership of benefit income. Another was their desire to preserve its identity as money for the *family*. Some feared that if the principle of *individual* ownership was introduced, then men might exercise this entitlement to the detriment of the family. Despite the fact that a number of women interviewed clearly placed a value on having an independent source of income, the study did not reveal a significant spontaneous demand among women for Income Support/income-related Jobseeker's Allowance to be paid to them as the claimant. However, the sizeable minority who did favour this included, significantly, three of the five women in the most inegalitarian group. This suggests that the availability of this option could be important for a minority of women.

Under the equal treatment rules, introduced under the Social Security Act 1986, couples were given a free choice as to which partner makes the claim for Income Support. In 1990, 5 per cent of all couples claiming had designated the woman as claimant, and this had increased to 10 per cent by 1996. By 1997, women claimed Income Support in 13 per cent of couples claiming, and income-based Jobseeker's Allowance in 6 per cent (statistics supplied by DSS to Patricia Hewitt, MP). Although it has always been the case that the claimant had to be the person available for work (unless the partner could claim on other grounds, such as caring for an elderly relative), our respondents suggested that the change in the title to 'Jobseeker's Allowance' underlined this even more strongly. This has been reinforced by the progressive tightening up of the availability and 'actively seeking work' rules in recent years.

Couples' chances of moving off income-related Jobseeker's Allowance might improve if the woman were to be the claimant and therefore the main 'job-seeker', given current labour market trends. The 1998 Budget proposed that the partners of unemployed claimants should be given help to seek work (in the case of childless partners aged under 25 as part of the New Deal). This was headlined in *The Independent* (19 March 1998) as the 'end of the male breadwinner'. Our study suggests that, while helpful in promoting greater gender equality, this approach needs to be sensitive to women's and men's investment in a more traditional male breadwinner model of the family and to the implications for both male and female identities of challenging this too directly. At the same time, about a third of men and over half of women interviewed favoured a model in which income was derived from a combination of men and women's earnings and a number of the women did emphasise the importance of earning in their own right. A more flexible benefits system, that facilitated a dual earner model and made it easier to take part-time work, might better suit some couples on benefit and make it more likely that they would be able to get off benefit altogether. Greater flexibility would give couples more room for manoeuvre and help them to adapt their working patterns to a changing labour market. At present, the evidence suggests that the rules imposed an inflexibility that was out of tune with some couples' need for more flexible arrangements. This inflexibility will have to be removed if the new policy announced in the Budget is to be effective. In addition, there was some indication in our study of a need for better advice and information in this area.

One policy option, designed to ensure that women receive some of the benefit income, would be to split the Income Support/income-related Jobseeker's Allowance payment between partners. An Equal Opportunities Commission research report, for instance, argued that this would 'significantly increase the independent incomes of women who previously had very low incomes' (Duncan *et al*, 1994, p22). More recently, it has been reported that the Social Security Secretary might be considering such a scheme (*The Independent*, 12 June 1997). Both previous research and our study show that families on benefit tend to operate a whole wage system, and splitting payments therefore might be counterproductive if the man treated his share as personal spending money and his partner's as money to meet collective expenditure while she retained the same expenditure responsibilities. Some of the respondents did indeed fear that this would happen. Certainly, this study provided little support for this reform as an effective way of enhancing women's economic independence. Nevertheless, it does indicate that it should exist as an option that a claimant's partner (usually the woman) can activate where she feels that this would better meet her and her children's needs. It is also possible that the women might have been more enthusiastic about the split benefit scenario had it included payment of all the children's share to them, given the importance attached to benefits for children being paid direct to the caring parent. Alternatively, this approach might increase the risk of men treating all of their share as personal spending money.

Overall, the study provides little support for the individualisation of Income Support/income-related Jobseeker's Allowance. However, in the two cases where the woman had experience of receiving a non-means tested benefit in her own right, it did appear that this was something that they valued. The interview schedule did not explore this avenue of questioning, as it would have complicated the already complex hypothetical questions even further. Further research is needed which examines whether views about individual payment of benefits would be different in the context of individually-based entitlement to benefit and where benefits are not means-tested.

In conclusion, despite some respondents' disclaimers, the way wages and benefit income functioned in practice confirmed the salience of the source and the recipient of income for control over its allocation. The study demonstrated unequivocally that the primary responsibility women undertake for prioritising the needs of children has not changed. Among these couples, benefit paid directly to women was allocated by them to collective family needs. The findings caution care, therefore, in devising policies for the payment of social security to families with children. Such policies should avoid both a limiting of the flexibility available to couples as they try to combine the demands of paid work and family life, and any reduction in the money available directly to women to meet the needs of their families. As policies are devised for what Mrs Hawley described as the 'hornets' nest' of household income distribution, it is hoped that this study will provide some insight into the dynamics of what happens within households in receipt of the two main means-tested benefits and how both women and men perceive them.

References

Bradshaw J and Holmes H (1989) *Living on the Edge*. London: Tyneside CPAG. London: Stationery Office/SPRU

Bradshaw J and Stimson C (1997) *Using Child Benefit in the Family Budget*. London: The Stationery Office/SPRU

Duncan A, Giles C and Webb S (1994) *Social Security Reform and Women's Independent Incomes*. Manchester: Equal Opportunities Commission

Esam P and Berthoud R (1991) *Independent Benefits for Men and Women*. London: PSI

European Commission (1997) *Modernising and Improving Social Protection in the European Union*. Com (97) 102. Brussels: European Commission

Goffman E (1990) *Stigma: Notes on the management of spoiled identity*. Harmondsworth: Penguin (originally 1963, Englewood Cliffs, NJ)

Graham H (1987) 'Being Poor: perceptions and coping strategies of lone mothers'. In J Brannen and G Wilson (eds) *Give and Take in Families*. London: Allen and Unwin

Hunt P (1980) *Gender and Class Consciousness*. London: Macmillan

Kempson E (1996) *Life on a Low Income*. York: JRF

Laurie H and D Rose (1994) 'Divisions and allocations within households'. In N Buck *et al* (eds) *Changing Households: the BHPS 1990 to 1992*. Colchester: ESRC Research Centre on Micro-Social Change

Lister R (1992) *Women's Economic Dependency and Social Security.* Manchester: Equal Opportunities Commission

Meadows P (1997) 'The integration of taxes and benefits for working families with children'. *Policy Options.* York: JRF

Mendelson M (1998) *The WIS that was. Replacing the Canadian Working Income Supplement.* York: JRF

Middleton S, Ashworth K and Braithwaite I (1997) *Small Fortunes: Spending on children, childhood poverty and parental sacrifice.* York: JRF

Millar J, Webb S and Kemp M (1997) *Combining Work and Welfare.* York: JRF

Morris L (1984) 'Redundancy and patterns of household finance'. *Sociological Review,* 33, 3, 492–523

Morris L and Ruane S (1989) *Household Finance Management and the Labour Market.* Aldershot: Gower

Pahl J (1980) 'Patterns of money management within marriage'. *Journal of Social Policy,* 9(3), 313–335

Pahl J (1989) *Money and Marriage.* London: Macmillan

Roll J (1991) *What is a Family?* London: Family Policy Studies Centre

Smith S (1991) *Economic Policy and the Division of Income within the Family.* London: Institute for Fiscal Studies

Thomson K (1995) 'Working Mothers: Choice or circumstance?' In R Jowell, J Curtice, A Park, L Brook and D Ahrendt (1995) *British Social Attitudes, the 12th report.* Aldershot: Gower

Vogler C (1994) 'Money in the Household'. In A Anderson, F Bechhofer and J Gershuny (eds) *The Social and Political Economy of the Household.* Oxford: OUP

Vogler C and Pahl J (1993) 'Social and economic change and the organisation of money in marriage'. *Work, Employment and Society,* 7, 1, 71–95

Vogler C and Pahl J (1994) 'Money, power and inequality within marriage'. *Sociological Review,* May

Walker R and Wiseman M (1997) *An Earned Income Tax Credit for Britain: Possibilities and Alternatives.* Loughborough: CRSP

Wilson G (1987) *Money in the Family.* Aldershot: Avebury